W9-CFH-483

Apple Pro Training Series

QuickTime Pro Quick-Reference Guide

Brian Gary, Steve Martin, and Jem Schofield

Apple
Certified

Apple Pro Training Series: QuickTime Pro Quick-Reference Guide
Brian Gary, Steve Martin, and Jem Schofield
Copyright © 2007 Jem Schofield

Published by Peachpit Press. For information on Peachpit Press books, contact:

Peachpit Press
www.peachpit.com
To report errors, please send a note to errata@peachpit.com
Peachpit Press is a division of Pearson Education

ISBN 0-321-44248-2

9 8 7 6 5 4 3 2 1

Printed and bound in the United States of America

Contents at a Glance

Chapter 1   Getting Started with QuickTime Pro 1
Chapter 2   Exporting Movies 19
Chapter 3   Editing Movies 37
Chapter 4   Creating Interactive Movies. 59
Chapter 5   Delivering Movies. 79
Appendix A   Codec Central 99
Appendix B   Internet Resources 103
Appendix C   QuickTime Player Quick Start. 105
Appendix D   QuickTime Preferences. 111

Glossary 127
Index. 133

Table of Contents

Chapter 1 Getting Started with QuickTime Pro 1

About QuickTime Pro 2

Playing Movies 3

Recording Movies 9

Saving Movies 14

Sharing Movies 15

Chapter 2 Exporting Movies 19

Exporting for the iPod with Video in

Five Easy Steps. 20

Exporting for Apple TV 21

Exporting Using the Animation Codec 22

Exporting Using H.264. 26

Exporting a Still Image. 30

Exporting an Image Sequence 31

Exporting Audio to 48 kHz AIFF 32

Exporting Using AAC. 33

Podcasting with AAC 34

Using Third-Party Codecs 34

Chapter 3 Editing Movies. 37

Displaying Movie Information 38

Displaying Movie Properties .38

Working with Movie Properties 40

Working with Movie Tracks. .42

Basic Editing 50

Chapter 4 Creating Interactive Movies 59
Using Tracks 60
Autoloading Web Pages 60
Creating a Clickable Web Link 64
Creating Chapter Tracks. 68
Working with Custom Skins .70
Creating Slideshows from Image Sequences 76

Chapter 5 Delivering Movies 79
Using Progressive Download .80
Using Real-Time Streaming. .81
Adding a Hint Track Automatically 84
Delivering to Cellular Phones 88
Using QuickTime Broadcaster (Macintosh). 95

Appendix A Codec Central 99

Appendix B Internet Resources. 103

Appendix C QuickTime Player Quick Start 105
Using QuickTime Player 105
Choosing Present Movie Options 106
Using A/V Controls 107
Upgrading to QuickTime Pro 108
Keyboard Shortcuts 110

Appendix D QuickTime Preferences. 111
Using Player Preferences. 112
Using QuickTime Preferences 117

Glossary 127
Index. 133

1
Getting Started with QuickTime Pro

QuickTime is much more than a digital media player. It's also a software architecture that other applications, such as Final Cut Pro, can use to drive multimedia functions. As a software architecture QuickTime comes with its own suite of applications, including QuickTime Player (with browser plug-in), QuickTime Pro, QuickTime Broadcaster, QuickTime Streaming Server, MPEG-2 Playback Component, and Darwin Streaming Server. Together they let you create, deliver, and play multimedia content. Additional components from third-party developers extend the capabilities of QuickTime even further.

This book focuses on how to use QuickTime Pro for a broad range of multimedia tasks. Whether you're an experienced media producer or a QuickTime newcomer, you'll learn everything from producing content for the web and portable devices (such as iPods, Apple TV, and cell phones), to exporting movies from one format to another (transcoding), to prepping content for live broadcast. (For a primer on using QuickTime Player, the version of the software that's preinstalled on Macs and available for free download for PCs, see Appendix A.)

The screenshots in this book primarily show the Mac OS X version of QuickTime Pro except where the interface on the PC is different, in which case Windows screenshots augment the presentation.

About QuickTime Pro

This book assumes that you are running QuickTime Pro version 7.1 or higher.

> **NOTE** ▶ If you have not upgraded to QuickTime Pro, you will see QuickTime Pro's media-creation and editing features dimmed in the menus.

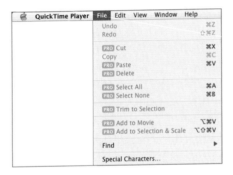

You can upgrade to QuickTime Pro in either of two ways:

▶ Purchase a QuickTime Pro license from the Apple Store online.

▶ Receive the upgrade when you install Final Cut Studio.

QuickTime Pro includes such features as direct recording, editing, and authoring capabilities; full-screen mode with floating playback controls; and the capability to save and export QuickTime content for a large number of codecs and formats.

> **NOTE** ▶ This book assumes a QuickTime Pro installation even when referring to QuickTime Player.

Playing Movies

QuickTime Pro is installed with a series of *codecs* (software that allows encoded movies to play back) that determine which movie formats you can play in QuickTime Pro. For example, the MPEG-4 codec allows you to play a movie from the web that was encoded using MPEG-4.

QuickTime files are like containers (or buckets) that hold media. As long as QuickTime Pro has the appropriate codec installed, the media will play.

If you don't have the required codec, QuickTime Pro will present an error message.

Content encoded with RealPlayer or Windows Media requires the installation of third-party software to view (or hear) the media in QuickTime Pro. Fortunately, QuickTime has a plug-in architecture that allows you to install compliant software easily, enhancing playback and encoding functionality. (To learn about installing third-party codecs, see Chapter 2.)

Movie Playback Options

You can play movies in standard or full-screen mode, play single or multiple movies simultaneously, and change movie playback size. You can also display additional controls and information when viewing movies.

To view information about the current movie, choose Window > Show Movie Info. The information displayed includes the encoding format, frame rate, playback speed, data size, duration, and pixel size.

To adjust audio and video and to access playback controls during playback, choose Window > Show A/V Controls.

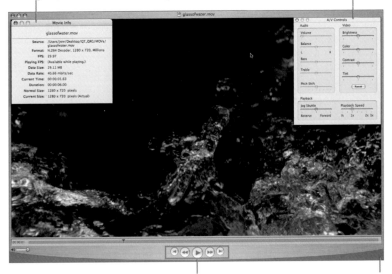

QuickTime Pro's player controls function like those on standard CD and DVD players.

To resize a movie, even during playback, use the drag handle at the lower right of the playback window. Press Control when resizing to maintain the movie's original proportions.

Standard Player Controls

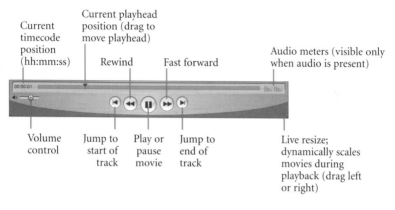

Current timecode position (hh:mm:ss)

Current playhead position (drag to move playhead)

Rewind

Fast forward

Audio meters (visible only when audio is present)

Volume control

Jump to start of track

Play or pause movie

Jump to end of track

Live resize; dynamically scales movies during playback (drag left or right)

Full Screen Mode

Any single movie can be played in Full Screen mode. This mode hides the menus, the desktop, and the A/V controls and is ideal for presenting movies to clients or for extended playback sessions. Though hidden by default, the A/V controls and the Movie Info window can be displayed in Full Screen mode.

The View menu controls the movie's playback size, along with playback options such as looping. Keyboard shortcuts let you activate these view options during playback.

In Full Screen mode, the application menu bar is hidden. Move the pointer to the top of the screen to reveal the menu bar.

To display the floating A/V Controls, move the pointer. You can drag the controls to any location on the screen. QuickTime Pro preferences settings determine how long the controls are visible in Full Screen mode before they return to their hidden state.

Full Screen Mode Player Controls

Volume control

Rewind

Name of movie

Fast forward

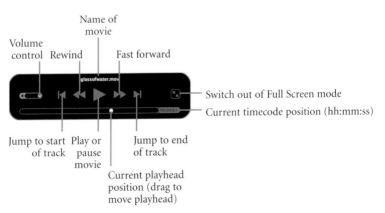

Switch out of Full Screen mode

Current timecode position (hh:mm:ss)

Jump to start of track

Play or pause movie

Jump to end of track

Current playhead position (drag to move playhead)

Full Screen Preferences for Windows

Full Screen preferences affect the default settings when you use QuickTime Pro's functions after choosing View > Full Screen or View > Present Movie. You can also choose when to hide playback controls in Full Screen mode. To open Full Screen preferences, choose Edit > Preferences > Player and click the Full Screen tab.

Choose the default size for movie playback in Full Screen mode. Choices are Half Size, Actual Size, Double Size, Full Screen, and Current Screen. For example, choosing Actual Size will always play the movie at its native resolution, as opposed to scaling it to fit the screen resolution.

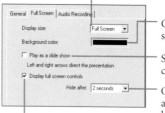

Choose the default background color that surrounds movies in full-screen playback.

Select to play in slideshow mode. A slideshow is controlled using the Left and Right Arrow keys.

Choose the amount of time that the player controls are displayed in Full Screen mode before being hidden. The range is from never to 10 seconds.

Specify whether player controls appear in Full Screen mode.

Multi-Movie Playback

Opening and playing multiple movies at the same time can be useful when, for example, you want to compare two versions of a clip that use different settings. In the following image, the original movie is displayed above a copy that has been modified using QuickTime Pro's Tint and Color A/V controls. You can make changes in real time while playing a movie.

You can also use this feature to compare identical movies with different codecs applied, and when viewing digital dailies, you can compare multiple takes of a scene.

Choose Loop to repeatedly play back a movie. This feature is useful to continuously view the original movie while changing the copy.

Play All Movies plays back all open movies at the same time. Processor speed, movie size, and other factors determine the real-time playback quality of the movies.

Original QuickTime movie; no changes.

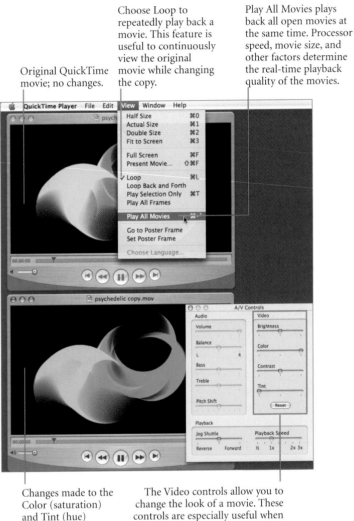

Changes made to the Color (saturation) and Tint (hue) settings of the copied movie.

The Video controls allow you to change the look of a movie. These controls are especially useful when experimenting with changes to a movie copy. These settings will not be saved with your movie.

To view the A/V controls, choose Window > Show A/V Controls.

Recording Movies

You can record simple audio and video in QuickTime Pro and have the content automatically encoded upon output. This is not as robust a feature as you would find in SoundTrack Pro, but it comes in very handy in some situations. For instance, if you're on the road with a laptop that has a built-in microphone or camera, you could create quick content on the fly with little effort or additional software.

Capturing Audio Only (Mac)

The first step in creating an audio recording in QuickTime Pro is to make sure that your input device is set correctly.

 — Choose QuickTime Player > Preferences.

When using anything other than a built-in microphone, select your microphone input device. This could be a USB mic, a mic routed through a FireWire input, and so on.

Make sure to choose your save location for the audio recording you're creating. If the recording is part of a larger project, be sure to save it with that project's assets.

TIP If your microphone does not appear in the Microphone pop-up menu, you may need to configure the device in the Audio pane of System Preferences.

Choose New Audio Recording from the File menu to start the process.

Checking your audio levels is important. If the meter is too low or high when you speak normally into the microphone, go to System Preferences and choose Sound from the Hardware category. Click Input and adjust the input volume.

Click the red Record button or press the spacebar to start recording.

When you're finished recording, click the Record button again (or press the spacebar) to stop recording.

When a movie has been recorded, it is immediately saved and can be played and manipulated just like a regular QuickTime movie.

Capturing Video and Audio (Mac)

The first step in recording a movie in QuickTime Pro is to make sure that your video and microphone input devices are set correctly.

Choose QuickTime Player > Preferences; then click the Recording icon.

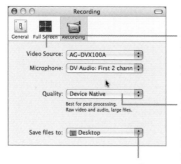

Make sure that you choose the appropriate Video Source and Microphone input settings. Here, a DVX100A is being used to capture video, and its built-in shotgun mic is being used for audio recording.

By choosing Device Native, you can capture at the camera's native resolution, which is 720 x 480 for a DV camera and 1440 x 1080 for an HDV camera. Other options will create a smaller MPEG-4 or H.264 movie.

Choose your save location for the new movie recording you are creating. If the recording is part of a larger project, be sure to save it with that project's assets.

TIP If you have a laptop with a built-in camera (such as a MacBook Pro with a built-in iSight camera), you can capture audio and video without having to connect any external equipment.

You can base your choice in quality on what you need to do with the content. For example, choosing Device Native from the Quality pop-up menu produces the highest-quality media that the device can create, a quality appropriate for ultimate editing on a platform such as Final Cut Pro. If you want to immediately upload or email the content, then one of the compressed formats (MPEG-4 or H.264) would be a better choice.

Choose New Movie Recording to start the recording process.

In the movie window that opens, click the red button or press the spacebar to start and stop recording.

Checking the audio level for a movie recording is just as important as checking the level for an audio recording. If the meter is too low or high when you speak normally into the microphone, go to System Preferences and choose Sound from the Hardware category. Click Input and adjust the input volume.

TIP With a third-party video camera attached to QuickTime Pro, you can capture content that you have previously recorded onto tape, drives, or tapeless media. This means that you can use the New Movie Recording command for more than just live recording. You can grab footage that has already been shot (by switching your camera to its VCR mode and playing back while recording) and then use that footage in your projects. Be sure to choose Device Native in your Recording preferences so that you capture at the camera's native resolution.

Capturing Audio (Windows)

Before recording, choose Edit > Preferences > Player Preferences to ensure that all the settings are correct for your hardware configuration. Then click the Audio Recording tab.

WINDOWS NOTE ▶ Video recording features are not available in Windows.

Click Choose to open Windows Sounds and Audio Devices Properties to enable the microphone input device. Windows lists all available devices in the Sound Recording > Default Device menu.

General	Full Screen	Audio Recording
Microphone:	Choose...	
Format:	QuickTime Movie (.mov)	
Save files to:	Desktop	

Choose the encoding format used when recording audio content. The formats are QuickTime Movie (.mov), AAC Audio (.m4a), and Uncompressed Audio (.mov).

Choose the default location for saving audio and video recordings.

When the preferences are set correctly, choose File > New Audio Recording.

Monitor your audio levels with the audio meter.

Audio Recording		
00:00:00		0.0 bytes

Click this button to start and stop recording.

Saving Movies

QuickTime Pro adds a few powerful options to the normal Save (or Save As) command that are worth exploring. QuickTime Pro can save two kinds of files: self-contained and reference.

Saving a movie as a self-contained file copies all the content into one file. Therefore, the size of the output file has a direct correspondence to the size of the source media. When you move the movie to another computer (or upload it to the Internet), all the media goes with it.

Reference movies contain only references to the movie's content (in relation to the content's current location in the directory path) and any metadata recorded with the movie. You can write reference movies almost instantly to disk because you do not have to copy any data, and you can thereby save considerable disk space. The downside is that if you move or delete any content referenced by the reference movie, you will make the entire movie unplayable. Additionally, if you move the reference movie without also moving all the referenced content (maintaining the exact directory structure), the movie will not play back properly.

TIP Final Cut Studio editors use reference movies often because the Final Cut Studio suite of applications treats reference movies the same as self-contained movies—enabling fast and efficient workflows.

To save a movie as self-contained or as a reference movie, first open the movie in QuickTime Pro and choose Save or Save As from the File menu. Then select one of the two options shown here and click Save.

Saving Movies from the Internet

You can download and save QuickTime movies directly from the Internet, provided that the movie's owner has enabled the movie for saving.

After a movie fully downloads, click the disclosure triangle at the lower right of the playback controls. If you do not see playback controls, most likely saving was disabled by the movie's owner.

About QuickTime Plug-in...

Open this Link

Save As Source...
Save As QuickTime Movie...

Plug-in Settings...
Connection Speed...

Choose Save As Source or Save As QuickTime Movie. When you choose Save As Source, the movie will be saved in its native format. Saving as a QuickTime movie lets you alter the output format.

NOTE ▶ Streaming content is not actually saved to your local computer. Instead, a small reference movie that points to the stream is saved, so you must be connected to the Internet and able to access the clip to play the movie.

Sharing Movies

The Share feature in QuickTime Pro lets you quickly email movies or post them to a web page using a .Mac account.

Exporting comprises an entire chapter in this book (Chapter 2), but the Share command offers a much quicker, no-frills approach to exporting—with the trade-off of limited options and delivery choices—and it works only on Macs.

Sharing to Email

The Email function under Share lets you encode a small-, medium-, or large-size version of a movie using the H.264 codec. You can also export in the native (or original) resolution, but doing so will most likely defeat the purpose of compressing for email delivery. After QuickTime encodes the movie, it will open your default email application and attach the movie to a new message.

Choose File > Share to open the settings window.

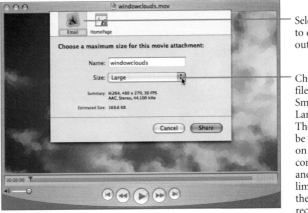

Select Email to display the output settings.

Choose from four file output sizes: Small, Medium, Large, and Native. The choice should be made based on the Internet connection speeds and any mailbox limitations that the sender or receiver has.

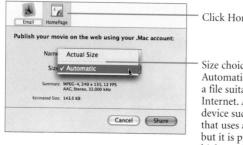

After the movie has been encoded, it will be attached to a new email message.

NOTE ▶Email recipients will need QuickTime Player version 7 or higher to play H.264 movies.

Sharing to HomePage

HomePage lets you share a movie directly using a .Mac account. The process is similar to that for the Email function, but you must have a .Mac account to use this feature.

Choose File > Share to open the settings window.

Click HomePage to display the settings.

Size choices are Actual Size and Automatic. Choose Automatic to create a file suitable for playing over the Internet. Actual Size is acceptable for a device such as an iSight or DV camera that uses a slightly higher resolution, but it is probably not suitable for a high-resolution source such as an HD camera. HomePage movies using the Automatic setting are compressed as MPEG-4 video. Actual Size movies are compressed using H.264.

When you click Share, QuickTime encodes the movie. If your Mac is connected to the Internet, it will upload the movie to your .Mac account, create a new page, and launch your default web browser at the site.

You can create a .Mac account from inside the .Mac pane of System Preferences.

2
Exporting Movies

The ubiquity of audio and video compression in all facets of production, post-production, and distribution makes both the QuickTime architecture and the container files it produces the best choices for cross-platform workflows. The flexibility of QuickTime Pro, with its standard installation of a wide array of codecs as well as the ability to use third-party codecs, enables you to not only play and save movies, but to export them in different formats.

Perhaps the most common use of QuickTime Pro is to transcode one media type to another—for example, to transcode a DV NTSC movie exported from Final Cut Pro to a high-quality H.264 movie bound for the web. All transcoding performed in QuickTime uses QuickTime's internal set of codecs (and any third-party codecs you have installed).

A basic understanding of codecs and the role they play in media compression is key to your successful transcoding from one format to another. Codec stands for COmpressor/DECompressor and refers to the process of compressing media from its original state with a set of instructions that another device can use to decompress the media and play it back. Each codec handles compression differently, with an engineering focus on the final output (encoding for the web is different than encoding for DVDs). For a primer, see Appendix A, "Codec Central," which describes all codecs installed with QuickTime Pro. Here are a few basic concepts:

▶ Compression reduces output file size but at the cost of quality. For example, if you start with high-definition (HD) source video and encode for the web, the output file will be exponentially smaller, but the picture quality will be drastically lower.

▶ The best approach is always to start with the highest-quality, highest-resolution, least-compressed footage and then convert downward. For example, you will get better results starting with DV NTSC video and encoding for the iPod with video than you will with that process in reverse.

▶ Choose your export codec based on your output destination. For example, if you want to encode for cell phones, choose one of the 3G codecs instead of the codec that matches your source video.

Exporting for the iPod with Video in Five Easy Steps

iPods with video display high-quality QuickTime movies in a very portable format. The advantage of using QuickTime Pro to encode for iPods is that you don't need to know anything about compression to successfully export a movie.

1   Open the source movie in QuickTime Pro.

2   Choose File > Export.

3   In the Save dialog, name the movie and select the destination.

4   From the Export pop-up menu, choose Movie to iPod. Notice that the Options button stays dimmed because you don't need to adjust any settings.

5   Click Save.

QuickTime Pro will encode your movie using H.264 for video and AAC for audio. The output file will adhere to the specification established for playback on iPods with video. The movie will have the file extension .m4v.

TIP This workflow is the base template for all other export examples in this chapter. By marrying these initial steps with an understanding of your desired output codec, you will quickly and easily harness QuickTime Pro as a transcoding platform.

Exporting for Apple TV

Using QuickTime Pro to export your movies for Apple TV is simple and easy. In fact, the steps are very similar to the steps presented earlier for exporting to the iPod with video. The resulting file will contain H.264 video with AAC audio both tuned for playback on Apple TV.

1 Open the source movie in QuickTime Pro.

2 Choose File > Export.

3 In the Save dialog, name the movie and select the destination.

4 From the Export pop-up menu, choose Movie to Apple TV.

As when you use the Movie to iPod preset, the Options button will be dimmed after you select the Movie to Apple TV preset.

5 Click Save.

Exporting Using the Animation Codec

The name *Animation codec* is derived from the codec's primary initial use by CGI artists, who needed a lossless codec to transfer media from one workstation to another. Use this codec if you're working in Film or CGI environments and want pristine video quality without regard for the resulting file size, but keep in mind that the high quality comes with the cost of increased file size. You should also use the Animation codec if you want the exported video to include an alpha channel (for working with transparency). Movies encoded with the Animation codec are very resource intensive and require robust workstations to achieve real-time playback.

The output quality of the Animation codec is inextricably linked to the quality of the source video: that is, quality will not miraculously increase during transcoding. Because the processing demands are so high, use the Animation codec only if you are starting with the highest-quality source video and need a lossless mechanism to transfer to another platform.

1   Open the source movie in QuickTime Pro.

2   Choose File > Export.

3   In the Save dialog, name the movie and select the destination.

4   From the Export pop-up menu, choose Movie to QuickTime Movie.

5   Click the Options button to open the Movie Settings window.

6   Click the Settings button.

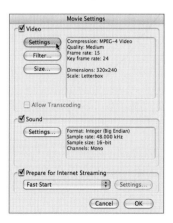

7 From the Compression Type pop-up menu, choose Animation.

8 In most cases, set Frame Rate to Current, so that the resulting rate matches that of the source media.

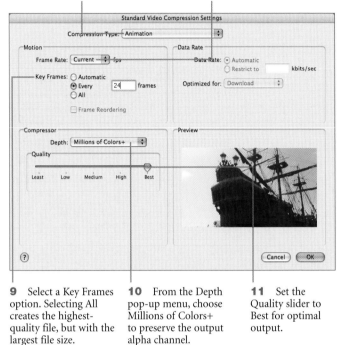

9 Select a Key Frames option. Selecting All creates the highest-quality file, but with the largest file size.

10 From the Depth pop-up menu, choose Millions of Colors+ to preserve the output alpha channel.

11 Set the Quality slider to Best for optimal output.

NOTE ► Selecting Automatic Key Frames in conjunction with a Quality slider setting below will let the encoder determine the best compromise between size and quality. You can also set your own keyframe frequency by selecting Every and entering a value in the frames field. The greater the value, the fewer the keyframes, resulting in smaller output files, but with reduced overall output quality.

12 Click OK to close the Standard Video Compression Settings window.

13 In the Movie Settings window, click the Size button.

14 From the Dimensions pop-up menu, choose Current. This is the best choice when encoding with Animation. Then click OK.

Export Size Settings

Dimensions: Current   690 x 388

☑ Preserve aspect ratio using: Letterbox

(if required)

☐ Deinterlace Source Video

Cancel   OK

15 If your movies are intended for playback only on a computer system, select this option to deinterlace the source video and ouput the movie with progressive frames.

16 If your movie has audio, click the Settings button in the Sound field of the Movie Settings window.

Sound Settings

Format: Linear PCM

Channels: Mono

Rate: 48.000   kHz

☐ Show Advanced Settings

Render Settings:

Quality: Best

Linear PCM Settings:

Sample size: 16   bits

☐ Little Endian
☐ Floating Point
☐ Unsigned

Cancel   OK

17 To maintain the highest audio fidelity, choose Linear PCM from the Format pop-up menu. Otherwise, you can add the audio encoder of your choice. Then click OK.

18 If you're using Linear PCM, you should match your output settings with the source media. For example, if the source rate is 48 kHz, set the value in the Rate field accordingly.

19 In the Movie Settings window, click OK.

20 In the Save dialog, click Save.

Exporting Using H.264

MPEG-4 Part 10, better known as H.264, is an interframe codec that produces high-quality video with relatively small file sizes. In comparison to MPEG-4 Part 2, H.264 can deliver up to four times the frame size while using the same data rate. This codec is also known as Advanced Video Codec, or AVC.

You can deliver H.264 content for both the web and high-definition DVDs. Use H.264 for the web if your audience runs the latest version of QuickTime Player (version 7 or higher) on relatively new hardware.

1 Open the source movie in QuickTime Pro.

2 Choose File > Export.

3 In the Save dialog, name the movie and select the destination.

4 From the Export pop-up menu, choose Movie to QuickTime Movie.

5 In the Save dialog, click the Options button.

6 In the Video section of the Movie Settings window, click the Settings button.

8 You can use the source video's frame rate by choosing Current from the Frame Rate pop-up menu, or you can choose one of the predefined values in the list. To manually enter a frame rate, choose Custom and then enter the value in the field that appears.

7 From the Compression Type pop-up menu, choose H.264.

Standard Video Compression Settings

Compression Type: H.264

Motion

Frame Rate: 15 fps

Key Frames: ◯ Automatic
◉ Every [   ] frames
◯ All

☑ Frame Reordering

Data Rate

Data Rate: ◉ Automatic
◯ Restrict to [   ] kbits/sec

Optimized for: Download

Compressor

Quality

Least Low Medium High Best

Encoding: ◉ Best quality (Multi-pass)
◯ Faster encode (Single-pass)

Preview

Cancel   OK

9 Set a Key Frames value manually by selecting Every and entering a value in the field. The greater the number, the fewer the keyframes, and vice versa. Optionally, select Automatic to let QuickTime determine the best number of keyframes based on its analysis of the source media, or select All to create a keyframe from every frame, producing pristine quality and very large output file sizes.

10 Unless you have a specific target bandwidth, select Automatic for Data Rate. With this selection, the encoder controls the size-versus-quality compromise based on where you set the Quality slider. Best creates high-quality files with large file sizes, Least creates the smallest files with the lowest quality, and settings in between split the difference.

11 With Frame Reordering selected, the output file will require more processing power during playback. For delivery to less powerful devices and systems (such as iPods and cell phones), deselect this option.

12 Unless speed is a paramount concern, always select "Best quality (Multi-pass)" for H.264 encoding. This allows QuickTime to analyze the source media before the compression pass.

13 Click OK when you have completed your adjustments.

NOTE ▸ H.264, like MPEG-4, employs an interframe compression scheme. Keyframes hold all the image data, and delta frames contain the interpreted image information between the keyframes. Frame reordering allows the delta frames to look to any keyframe in the movie for relative information, allowing H.264 to encode high-quality media very efficiently.

14 In the Movie Settings window, click the Size button.

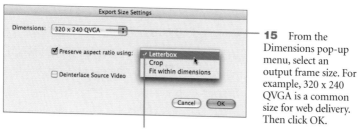

15 From the Dimensions pop-up menu, select an output frame size. For example, 320 x 240 QVGA is a common size for web delivery. Then click OK.

16 If your source frame size has an aspect ratio different from your output dimensions, you can preserve the source aspect ratio by selecting the Preserve Aspect Ratio Using box and choosing an option from the pop-up menu that will best display your content.

17 In the Sound section of the Movie Settings window, click the Settings button.

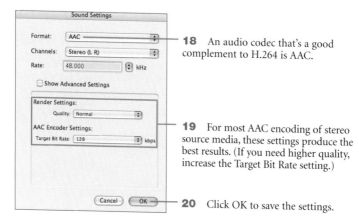

18 An audio codec that's a good complement to H.264 is AAC.

19 For most AAC encoding of stereo source media, these settings produce the best results. (If you need higher quality, increase the Target Bit Rate setting.)

20 Click OK to save the settings.

21 In the Movie Settings window, click OK.

22 In the Save dialog, click Save.

Exporting a Still Image

Sometimes you don't need to encode the entire source media: you need only a single frame to represent the movie. For example, if you are creating storyboards for a project, you can use a single image to represent an entire clip. QuickTime Pro easily produces the stills for each piece of media.

1   Open the movie in QuickTime Pro.

2   Park the playhead on the frame you want to export as the still image.

3   Choose File > Export.

4   From the Export pop-up menu, choose Movie to Picture.

5   Click the Options button.

6   From the "Compression type" pop-up menu, select an encoder. Photo – JPEG is a good all-around codec to use for still images. If you need the best possible quality, you can export using TIFF.

7   Use the Quality slider to set the level of compression. Best produces the least-compressed files with the largest file sizes, and Least produces the smallest files with the lowest quality.

8   Click OK to save the changes.

9   Name and select a destination for the output file and then click Save.

Exporting an Image Sequence

For certain CGI work, you may need all the frames of a movie exported as stills. The process in QuickTime Pro is very similar to that for exporting a single image, with a few exceptions:

1   Follow steps 1 through 3 in the preceding exercise.

2   From the Export pop-up menu, choose Movie to Image Sequence.

3   Click the Options button.

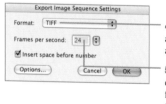

4   From the Format pop-up menu, choose a high-quality, uncompressed option such as TIFF.

5   Set the number of frames you want exported per second. If you want every frame, enter the source media frame rate in the field. Then click OK.

6   Image sequences produce a large number of files, so it's best to create a folder to hold them all instead of saving them to the desktop or the root of your hard drive.

7   Give the export a name. QuickTime Pro will use the export name combined with the frame number to uniquely label all the frame files. Then click Save.

Exporting Audio to 48 kHz AIFF

The sampling rate of an audio stream specifies how often analog audio is monitored and converted to digital information. Most sequences in Final Cut Pro have their audio sampled at 16-bit 48 kHz. All audio CDs are sampled at 16-bit 44.1 kHz, and MP3 files downloaded from the web can be sampled at as low as 32 kHz. You can use QuickTime Pro to easily produce sampled audio at a Final Cut Pro–friendly rate.

1 Open an audio file sampled at 44.1 kHz in QuickTime Pro.

2 Choose File > Export.

3 From the Export pop-up menu, choose Sound to AIFF.

4 Click the Options button.

5 From the Format pop-up menu, choose Linear PCM.

6 Match the Channels pop-up menu setting to the source media.

7 Set Rate to 48 kHz.

8 Set Quality to Best.

9 Set "Sample size" to 16 bits. Then click OK.

10 Name and save the file.

Exporting Using AAC

By default, when iTunes encodes an audio CD in your iTunes library, it uses Advanced Audio Coding (AAC) as the codec. AAC also works very well as an efficient encoder for audio bound for the web. You can use QuickTime Pro to transcode audio sources using the same high-quality compression as iTunes with even greater control of the encoder's settings.

1 Open a QuickTime-compatible audio file in QuickTime Pro.

2 Choose File > Export.

3 From the Export pop-up menu, choose Movie to MPEG-4.

4 Click the Options button.

5 Click the Audio tab to display the encoder's audio settings.

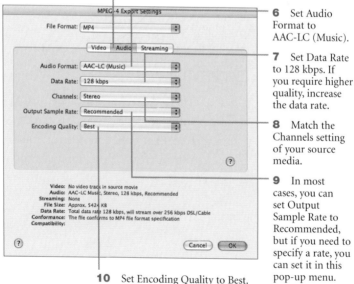

6 Set Audio Format to AAC-LC (Music).

7 Set Data Rate to 128 kbps. If you require higher quality, increase the data rate.

8 Match the Channels setting of your source media.

9 In most cases, you can set Output Sample Rate to Recommended, but if you need to specify a rate, you can set it in this pop-up menu.

10 Set Encoding Quality to Best. Then click OK.

11 Name and save the file.

Podcasting with AAC

You can easily translate the previous AAC steps into an audio podcast workflow:

1 Create the podcast in an audio application that can export in either the .wav or .aif file format.

2 Open the audio file in QuickTime Pro and choose File > Export.

3 Follow steps 3 through 11 in the preceding exercise with the following possible adjustments:

▶ If your podcast is primarily voice, you can reduce the data rate to 96 with no noticeable loss in quality and achieve a smaller export file size.

▶ Setting Channels to Mono reduces the overall export file size.

▶ You can reduce the sample rate to 44.1 with no noticeable loss in quality and achieve a smaller export file size.

Using Third-Party Codecs

QuickTime is installed with a wide variety of codecs that service a large number of production, post-production, and distribution channels. Formats such as Windows Media (.wmv), RealPlayer (.rm), and Flash Video (.flv) require third-party software for encoding. Fortunately, QuickTime has a plug-in architecture that allows you to easily install software from third parties and export using the same techniques presented in this chapter.

For example, the Flip4Mac plug-in by Telestream adds Windows Media encoding to QuickTime Pro. When this plug-in is installed, the Movie to Windows Media option appears in the Export pop-up menu of the Save Export window. When you click the Options button, the Flip4Mac WMV Export Settings window opens and allows you to adjust the encoder settings.

Each third-party plug-in adds a window for adjusting the encoder. Consult the vendor's documentation for information on how best to set the options for your particular source media.

Before purchasing a plug-in, go to the QuickTime website to check for compatibility.

3
Editing Movies

QuickTime Player is often regarded as an application solely for playback, but QuickTime Pro can perform many basic editing functions easily and efficiently. For example, if you're on the road with a portable computer (Mac or PC) and you need to quickly add or delete content from a movie, you can use QuickTime Pro to define sections for addition or removal and then perform the edit. You can then save the file as a new file or use QuickTime Pro's powerful export function to transcode the movie in another format.

Displaying Movie Information

QuickTime Pro displays the most useful information about a piece of media it can open in one easy-to-read window: the Movie Info window. If multiple movies are open at once, the Movie Info window displays information about the movie that is currently the active movie.

To open the Movie Info window, choose Window > Show Movie Info or use the shortcut Command-I.

⊖ ⊖ ⊖	Movie Info
	Pirate Ship.mov
Source:	/Users/stevemartin/Desktop/Pirate Ship.mov
Format:	16-bit Integer (Big Endian), Stereo (L R), 48.000 kHz Apple HDV 1080i60, 1440 x 1080 (1888 x 1062), Millions
FPS:	29.97
Playing FPS:	(Available while playing.)
Data Size:	31.69 MB
Data Rate:	28.98 mbits/sec
Current Time:	00:00:05.00
Duration:	00:00:09.17
Normal Size:	1920 x 1080 pixels
Current Size:	1920 x 1080 pixels (Actual)

The Format section displays the frame size as well as the audio and video codecs used to encode the source media.

There's a difference between the Normal and Current frame sizes. Normal is the native frame size of the movie and Current is the size of the window in which QuickTime Pro currently displays the movie.

Displaying Movie Properties

You interact passively with a movie's Movie Info window, whereas in a movie's Properties window, you can directly manipulate the tracks that comprise the movie. A standard QuickTime movie contains separate tracks for any media assets plus a default metadata track. As you will read in Chapter 4, QuickTime movies can also have tracks that contain code, text, and even interactive skins. Each track also has a set of user-configurable properties that vary depending on the track type.

The movie's Properties window lets you add and delete tracks and adjust track settings. Whereas QuickTime Pro displays only one Movie Info window, for the current movie, it displays an associated Properties window for each open movie. When multiple movies are open, make sure that you're adjusting the tracks for the correct movie by checking the title bar at the top of the Properties window.

To open a movie's Properties window, select the movie and then choose Window > Show Movie Properties or use the shortcut Command-J.

Working with Movie Properties

The track adjustments you make depend greatly on the track's type, but the basic workflow remains the same: Select a track in the table at the top of the window, click the desired tab in the bottom half of the window, and then adjust the settings.

Changing the Movie's Name Without Changing the Filename

QuickTime allows you to change the movie's display name without altering the filename. This feature can be useful when file-naming conventions dictate a name that is more technical than descriptive—with a movie hosted on a server, for example.

1 Open a movie and choose Window > Show Movie Properties.

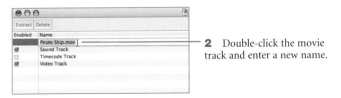

2 Double-click the movie track and enter a new name.

After you save the movie, the new name appears at the top of the player window, but the filename remains unchanged.

Displaying a Copyright Notice

QuickTime lets you embed a copyright notice into movies so you can brand your output media.

1   Open a movie and choose Window > Show Movie Properties.

2   Select the movie track and then click the Annotation button.

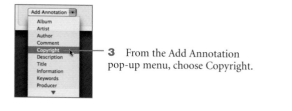

3   From the Add Annotation pop-up menu, choose Copyright.

4   In the Copyright row, double-click the Value field and enter your information.

5 Save the movie to preserve the changes.

6 To view the copyright information, choose Window > Show Movie Information, or press Command-I.

Working with Movie Tracks

Tracks let you quickly and easily manage the content in your movie. When working with tracks, remember that QuickTime files are just container files: buckets that hold data. As long as QuickTime Pro has the proper codecs, it can work with the data in the tracks.

Adding a Track from Another Movie

The Edit > Add to Movie command essentially superimposes or composites content onto an existing movie. In much the same way that video tracks work in Final Cut Pro, you can place one QuickTime track on top of another—superimpose them—to create a layering effect. This command differs from the Edit > Paste command, which extends the target movie's length by the duration of the pasted media—in essence performing the equivalent of an insert edit in Final Cut Pro.

The Add to Movie command takes clipboard content and places it in the target movie, so you must first have content loaded on the clipboard. The easiest way to load the content of an entire movie on the clipboard is to open the movie and choose Edit > Select All.

1 Select all of a movie (choose Edit > Select All) or just a portion (see page 46). Then choose Edit > Copy or use the shortcuts: Command-C (Mac) or Control-C (Windows).

2 In the target movie, position the playhead where you want the copied content's track to begin.

3 Select the target movie and then choose Edit > Add to Movie.

A new track is created in the target movie for each stream of content in the added movie.

4   Press Command-J to open the movie's Properties window and view the tracks.

In this example, the Fields movie was added to the Ocean movie. The Fields movie contains both audio and video tracks, so separate tracks for audio and video are created. Each track occupies its own layer; you can rearrange tracks and modify track parameters individually. The copied content enters the target movie at the timecode defined by the placement of the playhead.

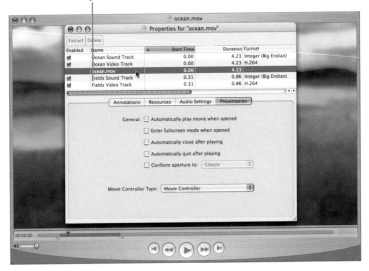

Using Add to Selection & Scale

Sometimes you may want to add content to a movie to make it perfectly fit the target movie's length. For example, you may want to do this when syncing music to a piece of video. Add to Selection & Scale composites a selection as a new track, just as Add to Movie does, but it also scales the video, audio, text, or graphic to the target movie's duration (or selection length if you define one).

The following exercise adds audio to a target movie.

1 Select and copy an entire audio file so that you can add and scale it to the selected part of another movie.

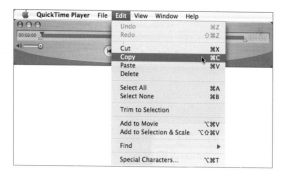

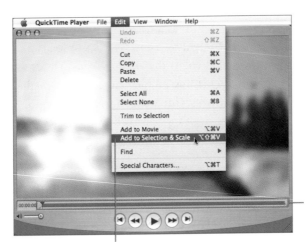

2 Set In and Out points to specify the portion of the movie into which you will add and scale your content.

3 Choose Edit > Add to Selection & Scale. When you add and scale audio to a movie, the audio speeds up or slows down to fit the selection, but the pitch does not change. This feature helps when you want to copy part of a video track and scale it to a smaller or larger selection area. This function also speeds up or slows down the video to fit the target.

In the movie's Properties window, the sound track has been added as a new layer and scaled to fit the area to which it was added—in this case, the entire movie.

Adding a Graphic Bug

You can brand your video content by using graphics or logos, also called bugs. Imported content enters the target movie on a separate track and behaves like a layer sitting on top of the existing media. In the Properties window, tracks with lower numbers are on top of tracks with higher numbers. That's why you always add the bug to the target and not vice versa.

Follow these steps to add a bug to a QuickTime movie using tracks in QuickTime Pro.

1   Create a graphic or logo to use as the bug.

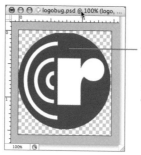

This bug was created in Adobe Photoshop as a simple logo graphic with text over a transparent background. It was saved in PSD format; any format that contains transparency, such as TIFF or PICT, is acceptable.

2   Choose File > Open File. Navigate to your graphic and open it in QuickTime Pro.

> **NOTE** ▸ Graphics open as single-frame movies in QuickTime Pro.

3   Choose Edit > Select All.

4   With the target movie selected, choose Edit > Add to Selection & Scale.

The logo graphic is superimposed over the existing video in the target movie as a new track with matching duration.

5 Choose Window > Show Movie Properties.

6 Select the logo track in the movie's Properties window.

7 Position the logo by using the Offset parameters.

8 From the Transparency pop-up menu, choose Straight Alpha Blend.

9 Use the slider to set the desired level of transparency for the logo.

QuickTime tracks with lower numbers in the Layer field of the Visual Settings display of the Properties window will appear ahead of those with higher numbers. If you want to adjust a track's visual placement, manually enter a value in the Layer field or click the up and down buttons to set the desired value.

TIP Save your project as a self-contained movie so that it does not reference external files.

Basic Editing

QuickTime Pro lets you perform fundamental edits on your media. This capability can prove helpful, for example, when you need to make fast, simple edits in the field or when you're working on a system without an editing platform, like Final Cut Pro.

The following exercises show you the most useful tools in the QuickTime Pro editing arsenal.

Working with Selections

Selections define areas of the media that you can then manipulate within the source movie or use as content to add to another movie. The following exercises demonstrate the actions you can perform after you've made a media selection.

1   Open a movie in QuickTime Pro.

2   Move the playhead to the start frame of your selection and then press I.

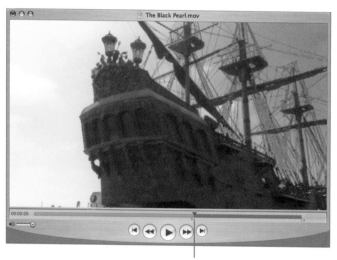

The In point marker moves
to the start of the selection.

3 Move the playhead to the last frame of the selection and then press O.

The Out point marker moves to the end of the selection.

TIP You can also hold down the Shift key while dragging the playhead to create a selection.

Playing a Selection

Before you do anything with your selection, you can audition it by choosing View > Play Selection Only and then pressing the spacebar.

TIP You can loop playback of your selection by pressing Command-L.

Jumping to the In or Out Point

If the playhead is positioned to the left of the In or Out point marker, press Option–Right Arrow key to jump to the marker.

If the playhead is positioned to the right of the In or Out point marker, press Option–Left Arrow key to jump to the marker.

Nudging a Selection

To move the In or Out point marker earlier or later in a movie (and so lengthen or shorten your selection), select either marker; then use the Left and Right Arrow keys to move it to where you want it.

Deleting Parts of a Movie

You can remove content from your movie in three ways: You can delete the selected portion of your movie, you can delete everything except the selected portion, or you can delete the selection and retain the content on the clipboard.

To delete the selected portion only:

1   Make your selection using any of the selection methods described previously.

2   Choose Edit > Delete.

To delete everything *but* the selected portion:

1   Make your selection using any of the selection methods described previously.

2   Choose Edit > Trim to Selection.

To delete the selected portion and retain the content on the clipboard:

1   Make your selection using any of the selection methods described previously.

2   Choose Edit > Cut.

> **NOTE** ▶ The overall file size of QuickTime movies edited using the steps presented here will not reflect the removal of media until you choose File > Save As and output the project as a self-contained movie.

Removing a Garbage Frame

Sometimes a movie has one frame that's undesirable—a garbage frame of black or white at the end of the file, for example. Instead of re-encoding the entire media, you can erase the one garbage frame with a few clicks.

1   Position the playhead over the garbage frame.

2   Choose Edit > Cut, or use the shortcut Command-X.

3   Save the movie.

Combining Movies

You can use QuickTime Pro to paste one movie onto the end of another movie, thereby combining the two. You can then save the results as a newly edited movie.

1 Open two movies in QuickTime Pro.

2 Select the source movie and choose Edit > Select All.

3 Choose Edit > Copy.

4 Select the target movie and move the playhead to the frame where you want to insert the source movie. (Often when you're combining movies, you will want to position the playhead at either the first or last frame of the target movie.)

5 Choose Edit > Paste.

6 Choose File > Save As to create a new QuickTime movie that is the combination of the source and target movies.

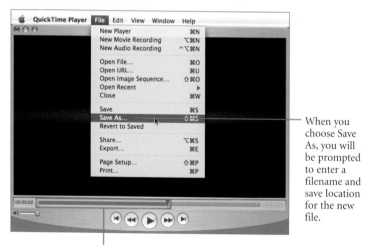

When you choose Save As, you will be prompted to enter a filename and save location for the new file.

After you choose Paste, the shaded section indicates that the selected movie has been combined with the target movie.

Performing Drag-and-Drop Edits

Drag-and-drop editing allows you to quickly drag movie content from one movie to another. For example, you may want to add an animated logo to the end of your movie as a *tag*.

The following exercise illustrates a quick way to tag your movies with content from another movie.

source movie   target movie

1 Arrange the windows for your two movies on your desktop so they appear side by side.

2 Select the movie that contains the source content.

3 Choose Edit > Select All or create a selection (see the preceding exercises) of the desired frames.

4 In the target movie, position the playhead at the end of the movie.

5 Click and then drag the source content onto the target movie.

6 When your cursor displays a green plus icon, release the mouse. The movie will be pasted (as in an insert edit) at the position of the playhead.

7 Choose File > Save As and then rename and save your project as a self-contained movie.

TIP You do not need to add movie content only to the end of a movie. Movie content is added wherever you position the playhead.

4
Creating Interactive Movies

QuickTime container files can hold much more that just audio and video. In fact, you can add entire layers of interactivity to your media. "Wiring" your movies transforms the audience's experience from merely watching the movie play to playing with the movie while watching it.

The exercises in this chapter present basic interactivity you can achieve with QuickTime Pro.

Using Tracks

A basic building block in the QuickTime architecture is the track. Tracks are linear assets containing samples that the QuickTime engine plays in succession. A sample can be a frame of video, a beat of audio, or even a command derived from a script.

The Properties window displays the tracks and their settings.

You can include nonlinear content in QuickTime tracks: for instance, Adobe Flash animations, scripts that open web pages, and text tracks that control movie navigation.

Video tracks contain a series of samples (frames) that can be played in a linear direction—forward or backward—along the timeline.

Enabled	Name		Start Time	Stop Time	Duration	Format
☑	Flash Track		0.00	4.77	4.77	Flash
☑	HREFTRack		0.00	4.77	4.77	Text
☑	Text Track		0.00	4.77	4.77	Text
☑	Video Track		0.00	4.77	4.77	H.264
	rachel.mov		0.00	4.77	4.77	-NA-

Autoloading Web Pages

You can actively script QuickTime media to open a new web browser window when it's playing via the QuickTime plug-in in a browser such as Safari. This scripting process is often referred to as *wiring*. For example, if your movie is a product demo, the web store could automatically open for the viewer at the end of the movie, or a team's highlight reel could open pages for its key players during playback.

1 Open a text editor that allows you to create plain-text documents (not rich text). You can use TextEdit on the Mac and WordPad on PCs.

2 Type *A<http://www.myurl.com/ >T<_blank>* (replacing myurl with the site name of your destination).

NOTE ▶ Syntax is very important, so be careful with case, punctuation, and spacing.

3 Save the document and open it in QuickTime Pro.

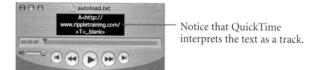

Notice that QuickTime interprets the text as a track.

4 From the File menu, choose Export (Command-E is the keyboard shortcut).

5 From the Export pop-up menu, choose Text to Text. Then click Options.

6 Select Show Text, Descriptors, and Time.

7 Make any adjustments to the timebase in relation to your output media. In this example, time is relative to the movie content at 30 frames per second. Then click OK.

8 Save the file and then open that newly exported text file in QuickTime Pro.

9 Open the target movie, the one that will launch the URL, in QuickTime Pro.

10 Create a selection (see Chapter 3) to show where you want the target movie to trigger the URL.

11 Select the open text movie and choose Edit > Select All (Command A). Then choose Edit > Copy (Command C).

12 Select the target movie. Then choose Edit > Add to Selection & Scale.

13 With the target movie still selected, choose Window > Show Movie Properties (Command-J).

14 Double-click the text track to highlight the text field.

15 Change the name to *HREFTrack*. Case and spacing are very important.

16 Deselect the Enabled box to hide the visible text of the track during movie playback. This change does *not* disable the code that launches the URL.

17 Save the movie.

Because the interactive portion of the new movie is activated only via the QuickTime plug-in, you will need to test the movie from a browser. Your audience (using Macs or PCs) will also need to have the QuickTime plug-in installed on their computers to experience this content.

Creating a Clickable Web Link

Instead of having a website open automatically when a certain frame plays (as you saw in the preceding exercise), you can create a visible link. When a user clicks the link, the linked URL will open in a browser.

1 Open a text editor that allows you to create plain-text documents (not rich text) and then select a font and text size.

2 Type the message that you want the audience to see in the target movie. For example, type *Click here for more info*.

3 Save the file and then open it in QuickTime Pro.

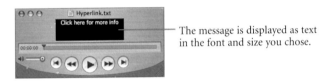

The message is displayed as text in the font and size you chose.

4 From the File menu, choose Export (Command-E is the keyboard shortcut).

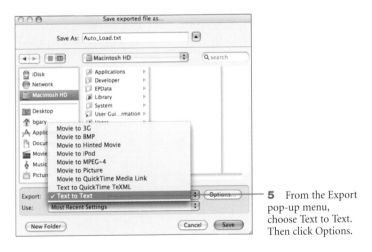

5 From the Export pop-up menu, choose Text to Text. Then click Options.

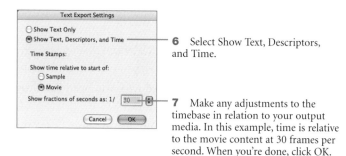

6 Select Show Text, Descriptors, and Time.

7 Make any adjustments to the timebase in relation to your output media. In this example, time is relative to the movie content at 30 frames per second. When you're done, click OK.

8 Save the file and then open that newly exported text file in your text editor. Notice that QuickTime Pro has added the descriptor and time information.

9 Change the width value to match the width of your target movie if you want the hyperlink centered on a black horizontal bar equal to the width of the target movie.

10 Directly before your custom text, type the code shown here, replacing the URL with your own. Be sure to enclose the entry with { }.

11 At the end of your custom text, enter the endHREF code to end the HREF command. Be sure to enclose the entry with { }.

12 Save the file and then open it into QuickTime Pro.

The text is now a hyperlink and will launch the default browser when clicked.

13 Choose Edit > Select All; then choose Edit > Copy.

14 Open a target movie in QuickTime Pro and choose Edit > Add to Selection & Scale.

The hyperlink appears in the entire movie at the top of the frame. Notice that the black bar is displayed across the entire width of the movie, as established in step 9. If you want a different size, you can readjust those pixel dimensions.

TIP If you want the link to appear only in a specific section of the target movie, define a selection before choosing Edit > Add to Selection & Scale.

To change the visual placement of the hyperlink within the target movie, choose Window > Show Movie Properties and select the text track in the table.

Adjust the X and Y offsets to alter the placement of the track. For example, if you want the link to appear at the bottom of the target movie, enter the movie's height in the Y field.

You can use the offset values to place the link below the source movie so that it won't cover any of the source media.

Creating Chapter Tracks

You can use QuickTime Pro to efficiently and easily add chapter markers to movies. Chapter markers enter QuickTime movies as tracks and are displayed to the audience as navigation aids in the QuickTime Pro interface to the right of the timeline.

1 Open a plain-text document in a text editor.

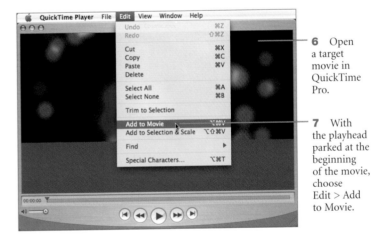

2 At the top, add the {QText} code.

3 Manually enter the timecode and name for each chapter, separated by a paragraph return. You do not have to use "Chapter"; you can use whatever descriptive text you like: for instance, "Lesson 1" or "All Star Game."

4 Save the file and then open it in QuickTime Pro.

5 Choose Edit > Select all and then choose Edit > Copy.

6 Open a target movie in QuickTime Pro.

7 With the playhead parked at the beginning of the movie, choose Edit > Add to Movie.

8 Open the target movie's properties by choosing Window > Show Movie Properties.

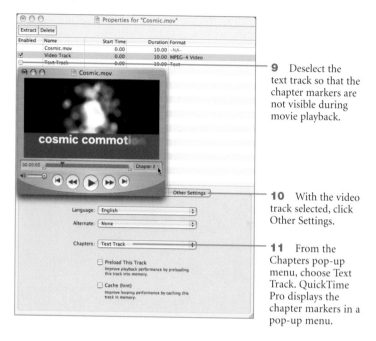

9 Deselect the text track so that the chapter markers are not visible during movie playback.

10 With the video track selected, click Other Settings.

11 From the Chapters pop-up menu, choose Text Track. QuickTime Pro displays the chapter markers in a pop-up menu.

TIP GarageBand lets you quickly add chapter tracks to QuickTime movies. Those tracks can be exported and played in QuickTime Pro. When using GarageBand, make sure to set your desired quality in the Movie Settings Export preferences.

Working with Custom Skins

You can use skins in QuickTime Pro to control the user experience, displaying your movies in custom windows instead of the default QuickTime Pro window. But QuickTime Pro skins let you do more than just decorate the player window: You can create custom controls and, because QuickTime Pro is fully scriptable, you can create interactive environments that match the look and feel of your content.

You will need to create the custom graphics for your skins in an application like Adobe Photoshop, and you will need to wire custom controls in an application like LiveStage Pro.

Follow these steps to add a skin to your movie:

1 Create the skin graphic and the two mask files in Photoshop.

2 Create a transparent window where the video will play.

Here a graphic with transparency (alpha channel) was created in Photoshop.

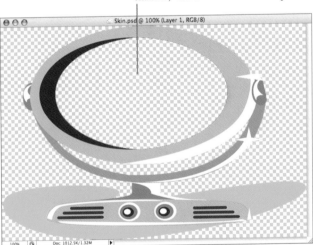

The window mask defines the visible player window. Areas in black will be visable, and areas in white will be left out of the final movie.

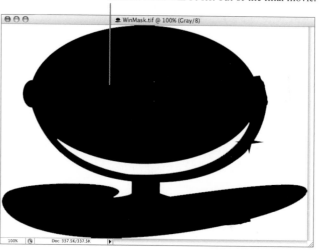

The drag mask defines the interactive area of the player window. Areas in black will be draggable, and areas in white will not be interactive in the final movie.

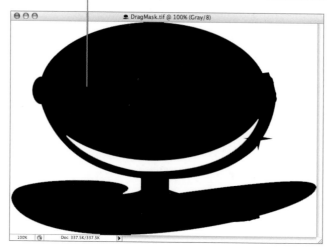

TIP If you want the visible area of the skin to be draggable, then the window and drag masks should be identical, so you can use two copies of the same file but with different filenames. If you want the draggable area to be different from the visible area of the skin, you'll need to create separate files that cater to each function.

3 Open both the source movie and the skin graphic in QuickTime Pro.

4 Select the skin and choose Edit > Select All.

5 Choose Edit > Copy.

6 Select the source movie and choose Edit > Add to Selection & Scale.

When first imported, the skin will cover the entire source movie.

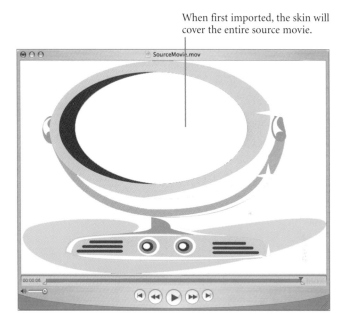

7 With the source movie selected, choose Window > Show Movie Properties.

8 Select the video track that contains the imported skin. If you imported the Photoshop file, the format will be Planar RGB. You can use the format column to help identify the skin track.

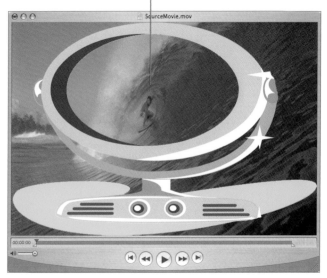

9 Click the Visual Settings button.

10 In the Transparency pop-up menu, choose Straight Alpha.

The skin's transparency now reveals the source movie behind it.

11 To adjust the position and scale of the source movie track, select
it in the Properties window and use the Transformation controls
to make the adjustments.

The goal is to have the desired
portion of the movie in the playback
area you created in the skin.

Use the Transformation
controls to make
adjustments

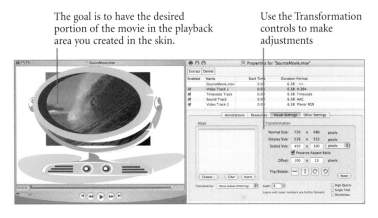

12 Save the movie as a new, self-contained file by choosing File >
Save As. For this example, name the new movie *Framed.mov*.

13 Open a text editing program and create a new plain-text document. Then enter the information shown here:

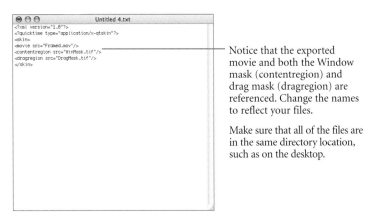

Notice that the exported
movie and both the Window
mask (contentregion) and
drag mask (dragregion) are
referenced. Change the names
to reflect your files.

Make sure that all of the files are
in the same directory location,
such as on the desktop.

14 Save the text document, but be sure to replace the .txt file extension with .mov. For this example, name the file *SkinXML.mov*.

15 Open the SkinXML.mov file in QuickTime Pro.

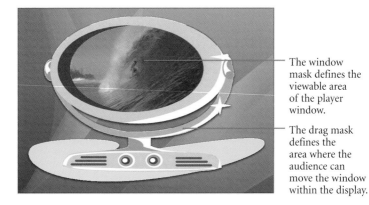

The window mask defines the viewable area of the player window.

The drag mask defines the area where the audience can move the window within the display.

16 Save the movie as a self-contained file by choosing File > Save As. Choosing this command saves all media references by SkinXML. mov in one file.

Creating Slideshows from Image Sequences

QuickTime Pro lets you create animated slideshows from a series of still images. For example, if you want to add some images to a presentation or broadcast some images on a website, instead of displaying them individually, you can have QuickTime Pro produce a slideshow movie. You can even add an audio track that plays as your slides appear.

To make your slideshow look right in QuickTime Pro, you first need to prepare your images.

1   Edit your still images so that they all have the same frame size, cropping or scaling the images as necessary.

2   Place all your images in a folder and give the images sequential numeric values. The image with the lowest number will be the first image that QuickTime places in the slideshow when it imports the folder; then it will place the rest in order.

3   Open QuickTime Pro and choose File > Open Image Sequence.

4   In the Open window, navigate to the first file in the sequence and click Open. It's important to select the first file in the sequence to ensure that QuickTime Pro imports all the files in order.

5   In the Image Sequence Settings window, choose a frame rate for the slideshow from the "Frame rate" pop-up menu. Then click OK.

Each still image will enter the slideshow in its own frame, so choose a value based on the amount of time you want each image to remain visible before the next image in the sequence appears.

6 Save the slideshow as a QuickTime movie by choosing File > Save.

You can use some of the skills you learned earlier in this chapter and in Chapter 3 to enliven your slideshows. For example, you could add a custom skin or a company logo; you can even add a soundtrack to the image sequence by following these steps.

7 Open a QuickTime-compatible audio file in QuickTime Pro.

8 Select the image sequence movie that you saved in step 6 and choose Edit > Select All; then choose Edit > Copy.

9 Select the audio file and choose Edit > Add to Selection & Scale. This command matches the length of the slideshow to the length of your soundtrack. Remember that because you're adding and scaling, the slideshow's duration will change. For example if you start with a two-minute slideshow and scale it into a one-minute audio file, the slideshow will play twice as fast.

TIP You can make the audio conform to the length of the slideshow by adding and scaling the audio to the slideshow.

5
Delivering Movies

QuickTime is a very flexible distribution container because it encodes multiple web-friendly formats, including MPEG-4 video, H.264, and AAC. (Chapter 2 provides detailed steps and scenarios for exporting your movies.) QuickTime media can be delivered over the Internet by one of two methods: progressive download or real-time streaming.

This chapter departs partially from the step-by-step methodology of earlier chapters, serving more as a primer for the digital distribution tools contained in QuickTime Pro. Each delivery project is different and presents its own unique challenges, based largely on the nature of the content being broadcast. Therefore, use the sections of this chapter to help you understand how these QuickTime Pro tools work and when to apply them to meet your delivery requirements.

A significant aspect of serving content on the web is just that: serving content. Configuring and administering a QuickTime Streaming Server is outside the scope of this book, but you'll see how to prepare your content so it can easily reside on QuickTime-based delivery platforms.

Using Progressive Download

Progressive download requires the least amount of server configuration of the Internet distribution methods because the delivery overhead is largely confined to the movie as played by the QuickTime browser plug-in and QuickTime Player. A progressive download begins movie playback as soon as enough data has been delivered to the client to ensure that playback will not be interrupted.

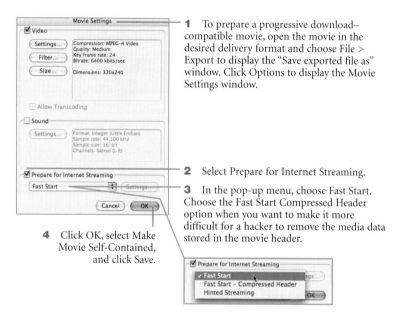

1 To prepare a progressive download–compatible movie, open the movie in the desired delivery format and choose File > Export to display the "Save exported file as" window. Click Options to display the Movie Settings window.

2 Select Prepare for Internet Streaming.

3 In the pop-up menu, choose Fast Start. Choose the Fast Start Compressed Header option when you want to make it more difficult for a hacker to remove the media data stored in the movie header.

4 Click OK, select Make Movie Self-Contained, and click Save.

TIP If your movie is already encoded in the delivery format, you can save time by choosing File > Save As and selecting "Save as a self-contained movie" in the Save dialog. This selection automatically prepares the movie for Fast Start Internet streaming.

Using Real-Time Streaming

The QuickTime Streaming Server uses the Real-Time Streaming Protocol (RTSP) to control the broadcast using the client's standard player controls: play, pause, fast-forward, and reverse. Streaming content is not downloaded to a user's computer, which makes streaming a good choice when you want to restrict content distribution. Streaming is also ideal for efficiently delivering long-form and live content.

All streaming media on a QuickTime Streaming Server requires a hint track, which tells the server how to package the data in the movie file. The steps for creating hint tracks for streaming movies differ depending on whether the delivery container is MPEG-4 (.mp4) or QuickTime (.mov).

If your movie is already encoded properly and you want to add a hint track, follow these steps:

1 Choose File > Export to open the "Save exported file as" window.

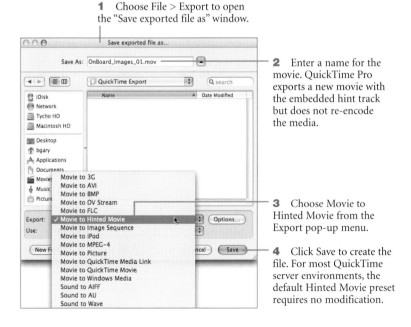

2 Enter a name for the movie. QuickTime Pro exports a new movie with the embedded hint track but does not re-encode the media.

3 Choose Movie to Hinted Movie from the Export pop-up menu.

4 Click Save to create the file. For most QuickTime server environments, the default Hinted Movie preset requires no modification.

To customize the hint track, click Options to open the Hint Exporter Settings window.

Self-contained media is much easier to organize on a server. Always select Make Movie Self-Contained unless otherwise instructed by the server administrator.

Select Optimize Hints For Server to enable the streaming server to handle the media more efficiently while streaming it to more viewers. The optimized output file size will be nearly twice as large, however.

By default, the settings are based on the source media; customize settings based on the requirements of your hosting environment.

To add a hint track while encoding media within a QuickTime movie container, follow these steps:

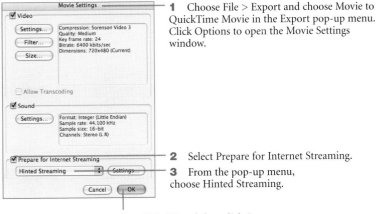

1 Choose File > Export and choose Movie to QuickTime Movie in the Export pop-up menu. Click Options to open the Movie Settings window.

2 Select Prepare for Internet Streaming.

3 From the pop-up menu, choose Hinted Streaming.

4 Click OK and then click Save.

You can customize the hint track by clicking the Settings button in the Movie Settings window.

Self-contained media is much easier to organize on a server. Always select Make Movie Self-Contained unless otherwise instructed by the server administrator.

Select Optimize Hints For Server to enable the streaming server to handle the media more efficiently while streaming it to more viewers. The optimized output file size will be nearly twice as large, however.

Click Track Hinter Settings to adjust the compressors and data rates for individual media tracks.

Adjust values based on the recommendations of the server administrator.

To add a hint track while encoding media within an MPEG-4 container, follow these steps:

1   Choose File > Export and choose Movie to MPEG-4 in the Export pop-up menu. Click Options to open the MPEG-4 Export Settings window.

MPEG-4 Export Settings

File Format: MP4 (ISMA)

Video   Audio   Streaming

☑ Enable streaming

Maximum packet size: 1450 bytes

Maximum packet duration: 100 ms

☐ Optimize for server

Video: None
Audio: AAC-LC Music, Stereo, 128 kbps, 44.100 kHz
Streaming: Enabled, max size 1450 bytes, max duration 100 msec
File Size: Approx. 64 KB
Data Rate: Total data rate 128 kbps, will stream over 256 kbps DSL/Cable
Conformance:
Compatibility:

Cancel   OK

2   Click the Streaming tab.

3   Select "Enable streaming." Make any adjustments based on recommendations from your server administrator. Selecting this option allows the server to handle the media more efficiently and stream it to more viewers simultaneously. The output file will be nearly twice as large, however.

4   Click OK and then click Save.

Adding a Hint Track Automatically

Apple introduced Automator with Mac OS X version 10.4 (a.k.a. Tiger) as a simple drag-and-drop interface for creating workflows by building them with the several hundred prefabricated actions that come installed in the Automator library.

Automator performs best when charged with performing repetitive tasks, especially those that require a series of manual steps to accomplish such as renaming all the files in a folder. QuickTime is both AppleScriptable and Automator ready, meaning that Automator has actions ready for you to build workflows for QuickTime right out of the box.

QuickTime Pro includes additional Automator actions that support the increased functions of the application. One of these scripts that you can build in Automator creates a hint track within QuickTime movies that are already encoded for the web. Here's a brief overview of the Automator interface:

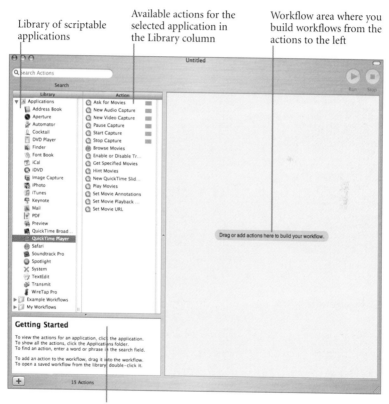

Library of scriptable applications

Available actions for the selected application in the Library column

Workflow area where you build workflows from the actions to the left

Description field that displays information about each action

Each new workflow opens in a separate Automator window.

To create a workflow that adds a hint track (for streaming media) to an already encoded QuickTime file, follow these steps:

1 The workflow will first need to know what files you want to hint, so drag the Ask for Movies action into the workflow area.

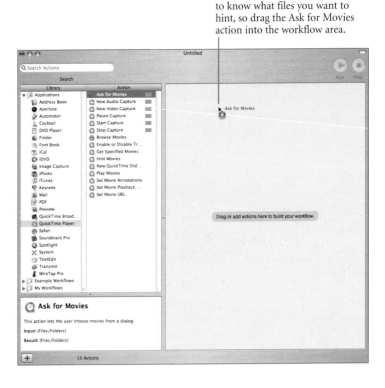

2 Add the Hint Movies action.

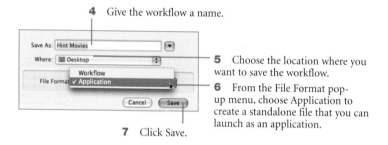

3 Choose File > Save.

4 Give the workflow a name.

5 Choose the location where you want to save the workflow.

6 From the File Format pop-up menu, choose Application to create a standalone file that you can launch as an application.

7 Click Save.

You can drag and drop movies onto the Automator workflow to execute the script, or you can double-click the application and navigate to your movies.

NOTE ▶ This particular workflow will not create new files; it will save the hint track in the existing file. If you want separate files, apply the hint workflow to a copy of your source media.

Delivering to Cellular Phones

In addition to streaming to computers via the Internet, you can produce and deliver content for cellular phones and mobile devices. The Third Generation Partnership Project (3GPP) protocol allows the creation of uniformly formatted content for multimedia cell phones used over broadband cellular networks. QuickTime Pro can encode audio, video, and text tracks for this protocol that are compatible with multimedia phones.

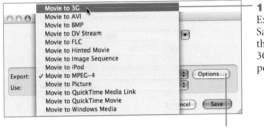

1 Choose File > Export to open the Save window and then choose Movie to 3G in the Export pop-up menu.

2 Choose Options to display the 3G Export Settings window.

3 QuickTime Pro exports content in several 3G-compatible file formats. Choose one from the File Format pop-up menu based on your target platform.

3G Format	Target Platforms
3GPP	Files for multimedia devices on GSM networks. Video can be encoded with MPEG-4, H.263, or H.264; audio can be encoded with AAC or AMR. Text is 3G timed text.
3GPP2	Files for multimedia devices on CDMA 2000 networks. Video can be encoded with MPEG-4, H.263, or H.264; audio can be encoded with AAC, AMR, or QCELP. Text is 3G timed text.
3GPP (Mobile MP4)	Files for multimedia devices using NTT DoCoMo's i-motion service. Video can be encoded with MPEG-4, H.263, or H.264; audio can be encoded with AAC. Text is 3G timed text.
3GPP2 (EZmovie)	Files for multimedia devices using the KDDI network. Video can be encoded with MPEG-4, H.263, or H.264; audio can be encoded with AAC, AMR, or QCELP. Text is 3G timed text.
AMC (EZMovie)	Files for AMC-capable devices using the KDDI network in Japan. Video must be encoded with MPEG-4; audio must be encoded with QCELP. Text is a KDDI format.

Within each 3G file format, QuickTime provides several export settings that can be customized to suit the content and the specific cellular device. Under the File Format pop-up menu is a row of five buttons: Video, Audio, Text, Streaming, and Advanced. Click a button to reveal the settings.

Choosing 3G Video Settings

In Windows, use 3G Export Settings to choose Video, Audio, Text, Streaming, or Advanced.

Choose a delivery format based on the table on the preceding page. Choose "Pass through" if the source media is already encoded properly.

Choose a compression type based on the table on the preceding page.

Set a data rate based on the available bandwidth of the network and the capabilities of the target device.

Choose an image size based on the display capabilities of the target mobile device.

Choose a frame rate that divides evenly into your source movie's frame rate. For example, if the movie is running at 30 frames per second, choose 15 fps.

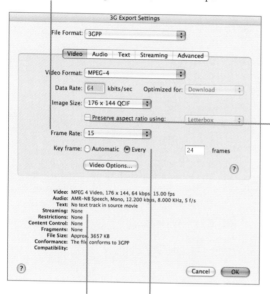

Preserve the aspect ratio of your movie when changing its size. When you select this option, also use the pop-up menu to choose a method for preserving the aspect ratio. Letterbox adds black bars to the top, bottom, or sides as needed and proportionally scales the source to fit the clean aperture. Crop scales, trims, and centers the movie to fit the clean aperture. "Fit within size" fits and scales the movie based on the longest side of the image. Crop and "Fit within size" generally are less desirable than Letterbox because they alter the source content.

The summary field displays the export settings on all five tabs.

Specify an exact keyframe interval by selecting Every and then entering a number in the frames field. Lower numbers increase the keyframe frequency for improved video quality but at the cost of increased file sizes. Select Automatic to let QuickTime Pro determine the best interval for the given source media.

Clicking the Video Options button displays one of two dialogs, depending on the format selected in the Video Format pop-up menu.

Video Format	Dialog
MPEG-4	**MPEG-4 Video Options** — ☐ Re-sync markers — (Cancel) (OK) Select "Re-sync markers" if your output will be streaming to multimedia devices.
H.263	The Video Options button is dimmed.
H.264	**H.264 Video Options** — Encoding Mode: ○ Best quality (Multi-pass) ◉ Faster encode (Single-pass) — (Cancel) (OK) Select the option that best suits your encoding need: quality (Multi-pass) or speed (Single-pass).

Choosing 3G Audio Settings

Choose the audio format based on the delivery format (see the table on the preceding page).

Choose the data rate and channels (Mono or Stereo) based on the delivery requirements (see page 89). Higher data rates produce higher quality and increase file sizes.

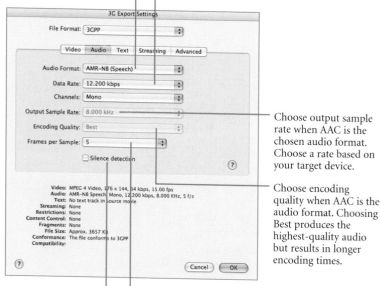

Choose output sample rate when AAC is the chosen audio format. Choose a rate based on your target device.

Choose encoding quality when AAC is the audio format. Choosing Best produces the highest-quality audio but results in longer encoding times.

You can select the "Silence detection" option only when you're using the AMR format. It lets the encoder detect silence in the stream and adjust the data rate accordingly.

Choose the number of frames per sample when using the AMR format. Set this option so that the number divides evenly into the video frame rate, and the two streams will encode more efficiently.

Choosing 3G Text Settings

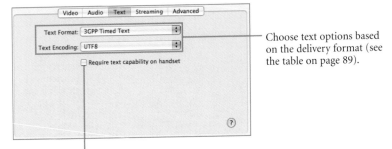

Choose text options based on the delivery format (see the table on page 89).

If you want only text-capable devices to view the output media, select this option.

NOTE ▶ If the source media does not include a text track, the 3G text options will be dimmed.

Choosing 3G Streaming Settings

Enable output media streaming.

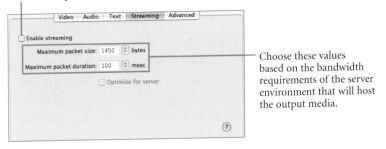

Choose these values based on the bandwidth requirements of the server environment that will host the output media.

Choosing Advanced 3G Settings

| Video | Audio | Text | Streaming | Advanced |

☑ Restrict distribution (effective only on handsets)

☐ Playback count: 3 times

☐ Expiration: ○ After 30 days

○ On 12 / 13 / 2006 ⊕ mm/dd/yyyy

☑ Fragment movie

Initial fragment: 15 sec

Subsequent fragments: 15 sec

These options establish distribution security protocols by restricting the user's ability to watch and copy the output media. They are available only for the 3GPP (Mobile MP4), 3GPP2 (EZMovie), and AMC (EZMovie) formats. Note that security setting are respected only by the phone and not by QuickTime Pro.

These options allow the movie to download in smaller segments, similar to progressive download, so media playback can start before the entire file is downloaded. They are available only for the 3GPP2 and 3GPP2 (EZMovie) formats.

Using QuickTime Broadcaster (Macintosh)

Although the QuickTime Streaming Server (contained in Mac OS X Server version 10.4) is outside the scope of this guide, Apple's free live-encoding software QuickTime Broadcaster lets you easily stream a live QuickTime feed to a direct one-to-one Internet connection. (You can also broadcast the feed over the Internet by sending it to a QuickTime Streaming Server.) If your system meets the minimum requirements, you can download and install QuickTime Broadcaster from the Apple website at www.apple.com/quicktime/broadcaster.

QuickTime Broadcaster can be useful when you want to stream either live or recorded content from one location to another. For example, if you are holding auditions for a movie and one of the producers cannot attend a session, you can send the live or recorded feed directly to the producer as a direct broadcast.

To create a direct one-to-one broadcast, follow these steps:

1 Attach a web camera (iSight, for example) to your Mac and launch QuickTime Broadcaster.

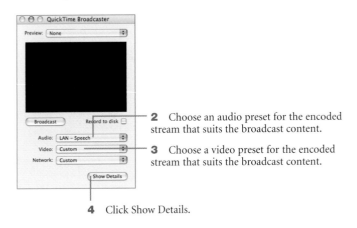

2 Choose an audio preset for the encoded stream that suits the broadcast content.

3 Choose a video preset for the encoded stream that suits the broadcast content.

4 Click Show Details.

NOTE ▶ For the Preview display, you can choose None, Source (the raw feed from the camera), or Compressed (the raw source with the applied video preset).

NOTE ▶ Select "Record to disk" to save the stream to disk.

5 Click the Network tab.

6 In the Transmission pop-up menu, choose Manual Unicast.

7 Enter the IP address of the receiving computer; you will need to get the address from the receiving computer's owner (or administrator if the computer is a server). The default value is your IP address.

8 Choose File > Export SDP.

NOTE ▶ SDP is an abbreviation for Session Description Protocol.

9 Email or FTP the SDP file to the person with whom you will have the direct connection. That person will need to launch this file in QuickTime to see the broadcast.

10 Click Broadcast in the QuickTime Broadcaster window.

11 On the receiving computer, double-click the SDP file to view the feed in QuickTime.

To broadcast using a QuickTime Streaming Server, use the preceding steps but with the following variations:

In the Transmission pop-up menu, choose Automatic Unicast (Announce).

Enter the host name or IP address.

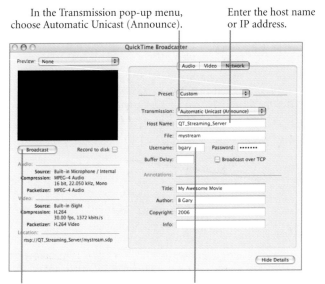

Click Broadcast. You do not need to create the SDP file; the streaming information will be sent to the server automatically.

Enter the user name and password required for broadcasting.

A
Codec Central

CODEC	APPLICATION	PROS	CONS
AAC (see Chapter 2)	High-quality audio distribution.	Achieves high audio fidelity while simultaneously producing relatively small output file size. Codec used by Apple to encode music for the iTunes store; also used by iTunes software.	Not as compatible as MP3 with playback software and devices.
Animation (see Chapter 2)	Motion graphics and high-quality video.	Includes an alpha channel; maintains source quality in uncompressed format and can also use interframe compression.	Very large output file sizes and requires high data rates. Demanding resource requirements for playback.
Apple Pixlet Video	Distribution.	Handles SD-to-HD video transcoding with flexible output settings. Good balance between compression ratios and quality.	High-level hardware requirements for rendering and playback.

CODEC	APPLICATION	PROS	CONS
Cinepak	Cross-platform delivery for Macs and PCs.	Venerable codec that will play on versions of QuickTime dating back to version 1. Good playback performance on slower systems.	Suffers from poor quality and large file sizes.
DV/DVCPRO – NTSC or PAL	Common format used by consumer and prosumer SD video equipment (such as MiniDV).	Highly compatible cross-platform codec. Works with most editing systems and video hardware.	Image data is compressed 5:1; color data is compressed 4:1:1.
DVCPRO 50	Professional-grade SD digital video from Panasonic. Similar in quality and frame size to DigiBeta.	Double the quality and color-space of standard DV.	Double the data rate and file size of standard DV for similar media duration.
DVCPRO HD	High-definition version of Panasonic's digital video format.	1080i- and 720p-encoding versions of the codec; lower bandwidth requirements than other HD formats. Can edit over FireWire in Final Cut Pro.	Has more intraframe compression than other HD formats.
H.264 (see Chapter 2)	High-quality distribution.	Very scalable, from cell phone delivery to HD DVD.	Less compatible with older computers and video equipment; demanding hardware requirements for encoding.

CODEC	APPLICATION	PROS	CONS
Linear PCM	Uncompressed production audio format.	Excellent lossless quality. Preferred format for many NLE systems.	Large file sizes compared to compressed audio formats.
Motion JPEG	High-quality offline production.	4:2:2 color space; all I-frame compression; spatial quality encoder.	May require third-party editing hardware.
MPEG-4	Distribution; used primarily for web delivery.	Compatible with QuickTime 6 and higher.	Higher data rates compared to other web delivery codecs.
Photo – JPEG	Lossless production.	Can employ spatial compression to reduce file size without noticeable loss in quality; 4:4:4 color space.	Does not have an alpha channel; hardware intensive.
Planar RGB	Lossless production.	All I-frame compression; includes an alpha channel; smaller output file sizes compared to animation codec.	Relatively large file sizes; no interframe compression.
Q-Design Music 2	Audio distribution tuned for music content.	Good quality for the level of compression; very compatible delivery format.	Audio fidelity not as good as with AAC.
Qualcomm Pure Voice	Audio distribution tuned for voice content.	Good quality for the level of compression; very compatible delivery format.	Audio fidelity not as good as with AAC.

CODEC	APPLICATION	PROS	CONS
Sorenson 3	Distribution; used primarily for web delivery.	Highly compatible with QuickTime versions 5 and higher; small file sizes in relation to the output quality.	Not as scalable as H.264.
TIFF (see Chapter 2)	Image sequence exporting.	Creates a separate file for every frame of source video. Common format used by animators and compositors delivering to NLE systems.	Can create thousands of sequential files depending on the duration of the source video.
Uncompressed 8/10 bit	SD production; often used for digitized analog sources (such as BetaSP).	High quality; 4:2:2 video at a 720 x 486 frame size.	Large output file sizes and high data rates.

B
Internet Resources

Apple

The following pages at the Apple website provide extended information and technical resources for both QuickTime Pro (the application) and QuickTime (the architecture).

- www.apple.com/quicktime/pro/mac.html
- www.apple.com/quicktime/technologies/
- www.apple.com/quicktime/resources/components.html
- http://developer.apple.com/quicktime/

Codecs

The following sites provide in-depth resources and information regarding the compression technologies discussed in this book.

- www.adamwilt.com/DV.html
- www.adamwilt.com/HDV/
- www.chiariglione.org/mpeg/
- www.compression-links.info/MPEG
- www.siggraph.org/education/materials/HyperGraph/video/codecs/Default.htm
- http://codecs.onerivermedia.com/

Third-Party Scripting Software

The following product sites provide information about software that allows you to add and control the interactive aspects of QuickTime and use scripting with greater precision than presented in the exercises in Chapter 4.

▶ www.adobe.com/products/golive/

▶ www.totallyhip.com/

▶ www.videoclix.com/videoclix_main.html

C
QuickTime Player Quick Start

QuickTime Player is a freely distributed, cross-platform (Mac and PC) multimedia application. This appendix describes basic QuickTime Player functions such as controlling media playback attributes and presents timesaving keyboard shortcuts.

Using QuickTime Player

QuickTime Player is a freeware digital multimedia player for Macintosh and Windows-based computers that plays video, music and audio, and QuickTime virtual reality (VR) movie files. It also allows you to view graphics and still images in a variety of formats.

QuickTime Player allows the live resizing of video content as it's played, it supports up to 24 channels of surround audio, and it provides extensive audiovisual controls that let you adjust such parameters as volume, pitch, brightness, and color. With the A/V controls, you can also select the overall playback speed and direction (reverse and forward).

QuickTime Player also includes zero-configuration streaming and a browser plug-in. Zero-configuration streaming automatically chooses the best online connection speed when you view streaming content. The browser plug-in lets you seamlessly view QuickTime-supported content on the Web.

Choosing Present Movie Options

Present Movie lets you control the playback of movies in Full Screen mode. This feature allows you to present a QuickTime file in other than the default configuration.

Choose View > Present Movie to display the Present Movie dialog.

Choose the movie playback size: Actual Size, Double Size, Full Screen, or Half Size.

Click to change the background color surrounding the movie. The default is black.

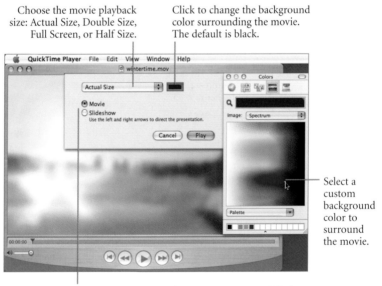

Select a custom background color to surround the movie.

Choose a Movie or Slideshow presentation. Slideshow allows you to step through images one at a time using the Left and Right Arrow keys.

Using A/V Controls

If you are using QuickTime Pro with Windows or with Mac OS X version 10.4 or higher and have a video card capable of core image processing, the A/V Controls window will display video options that let you adjust brightness, color, contrast, and tint. An additional audio adjustment, Pitch Shift, is also available.

Choose Window > Show A/V Controls to adjust the settings.

Adjust the overall audio levels (loudness). Volume changes made using the A/V controls or player controls are saved with the QuickTime movie. Changes to A/V controls other than Volume are not saved with movies.

Pan the audio left and right.

Adjust the tone of the lowest part of the audio range.

Adjust the tone of the highest part of the audio range.

Adjust the pitch of the audio without changing the tempo—great for making a voice sound lower or higher in pitch

Play the movie forward or backward at variable speeds.

Set the playback speed of a movie.

Adjust the overall luminance
(light values) of your image.

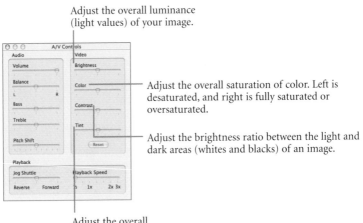

Adjust the overall saturation of color. Left is
desaturated, and right is fully saturated or
oversaturated.

Adjust the brightness ratio between the light and
dark areas (whites and blacks) of an image.

Adjust the overall
hue of the movie.

Upgrading to QuickTime Pro

You must have the latest version of Apple's free QuickTime Player
before you can upgrade to QuickTime Pro. The player is available for
Macintosh and Windows at www.apple.com/quicktime.

After you have downloaded and installed QuickTime Player, you
have two options for upgrading to QuickTime Pro. If you're using
a Macintosh, choose QuickTime Player > Buy QuickTime Pro; on
a Windows computer, choose Help > Buy QuickTime Pro. You can
also go to www.apple.com/quicktime and follow the Upgrade Now
instructions. Using these methods, you will be able to purchase your
QuickTime Pro registration code in the Apple Online Store.

You will receive a registration code via email; then you'll need to follow the instructions to install the QuickTime Pro registration key.

TIP Full installation instructions can be found at www.apple.
com/quicktime/pro/keyinstall.html.

On a Macintosh, you register QuickTime Pro using the QuickTime preferences on the Register tab. To perform registration in QuickTime Player for Windows, choose Edit > Preferences > Register.

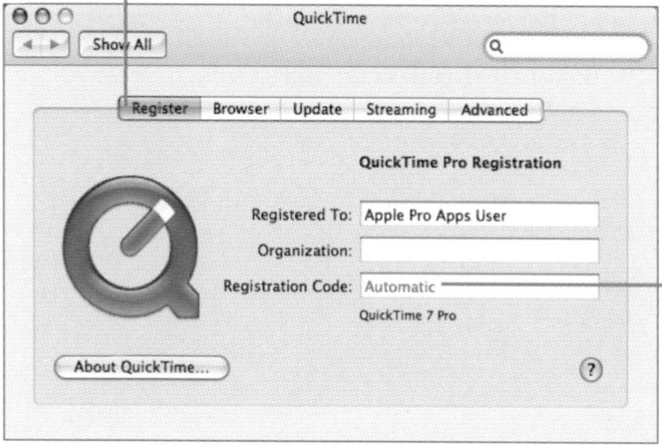

Automatic registration code entry for the Final Cut Studio version of QuickTime Pro is shown here. Other QuickTime versions require users to enter a registration code.

To verify that you've upgraded to QuickTime Pro successfully, look at the QuickTime Player menus. They should no longer display any dimmed options. This means that all the features of QuickTime Pro are now available.

NOTE ▶ After you upgrade to QuickTime Pro, your player is still called QuickTime Player.

Registration codes from previous versions of QuickTime Pro do not work with the latest version.

Keyboard Shortcuts

The following table presents keyboard shortcuts that you can use for your work in QuickTime. Macintosh shortcuts are shown first, followed by shortcuts for Windows.

Keyboard Shortcuts

Mac/Windows	Action
Command-O/Control-O	Open file
Command-L/Control-L	Loop movie during playback
Spacebar	Play and pause movie
Option–Left Arrow/Control–Left Arrow	Go to beginning of selection or movie
Option–Right Arrow/Control–Right Arrow	Go to end of selection or movie
Command-I/Control-I	Display Movie Info window
Command-K/Control-K	Display A/V controls
Command-F/Control-F	Toggle Full Screen and standard modes
Control–Left Arrow	Set maximum volume
Control–Right Arrow	Set minimum volume
Command-1/Control-1	Play movie at actual size
Command-2/Control-2	Play movie at double size
Command-3/Control-3	Fit movie to screen
Command-0/Control 0	Play movie at half size
Command-Return/Control-Enter	Play all movies

D
QuickTime Preferences

During installation, QuickTime generally optimizes the preference settings based on your current configuration, but you can easily customize the preferences to suit your specific system. You can access and change two sets of preferences within QuickTime Pro: Player preferences and QuickTime preferences. Player preferences control the way the playback application QuickTime Player handles incoming media for recording and outgoing media for playback. The QuickTime preferences control the QuickTime browser plug-in, allow QuickTime registration (turning QuickTime into QuickTime Pro), and set advanced systemwide file-type playback options. By adjusting preferences, you can take control of a wide variety of tasks, from increasing or decreasing the target bandwidth of streaming media to changing the number of default file types (MIME types) that will launch QuickTime Player.

Using Player Preferences

Player preferences are organized into three categories: General, Full Screen, and Recording. These preferences are specific to QuickTime Pro and allow you to control the overall functionality of the application.

General Player Preferences

General settings affect what occurs each time you open a new QuickTime movie.

WINDOWS NOTE ▶ To open General preferences, choose Edit > Preferences > Player Preferences and click the General tab.

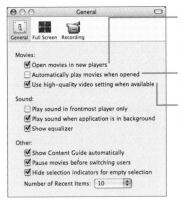

Select to create a new player for every QuickTime movie that is opened. When this option is not selected, the newly opened movie will replace the current movie in the player.

Select to immediately play movies when they are opened.

Select to play movies at a higher quality. This setting requires more processor capacity.

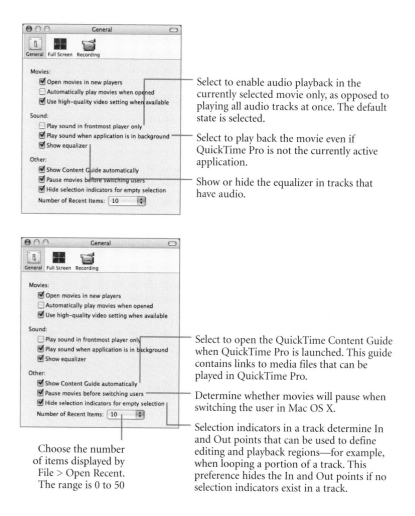

Select to enable audio playback in the currently selected movie only, as opposed to playing all audio tracks at once. The default state is selected.

Select to play back the movie even if QuickTime Pro is not the currently active application.

Show or hide the equalizer in tracks that have audio.

Select to open the QuickTime Content Guide when QuickTime Pro is launched. This guide contains links to media files that can be played in QuickTime Pro.

Determine whether movies will pause when switching the user in Mac OS X.

Selection indicators in a track determine In and Out points that can be used to define editing and playback regions—for example, when looping a portion of a track. This preference hides the In and Out points if no selection indicators exist in a track.

Choose the number of items displayed by File > Open Recent. The range is 0 to 50

Full Screen Preferences for Mac

Full Screen preferences affect the default settings for QuickTime Pro's functions when you use View > Full Screen and View > Present Movie. You can also choose when to hide playback controls in Full Screen mode.

Select the default monitor for full-screen movie playback. If only one monitor is attached to a system, there will be no option to choose.

Choose the default size for movie playback in Full Screen mode. Choices are Half Size, Actual Size, Double Size, Full Screen, and Current Screen. For example, choosing Actual Size will always play the movie at its native resolution, as opposed to scaling it to fit the screen resolution.

Choose the default background color that surrounds movies in full-screen playback.

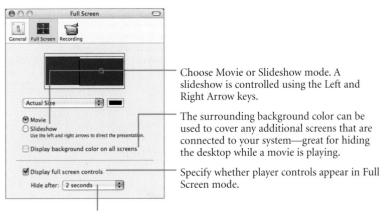

Choose Movie or Slideshow mode. A slideshow is controlled using the Left and Right Arrow keys.

The surrounding background color can be used to cover any additional screens that are connected to your system—great for hiding the desktop while a movie is playing.

Specify whether player controls appear in Full Screen mode.

Choose the amount of time that the player controls are displayed in Full Screen mode before being hidden. The range is from never to 10 seconds.

TIP Changes to the surrounding background color using the color well affect only movies played using View > Full Screen. To change the background color when using Present Movie, choose View > Present Movie and use the color well.

Full Screen Preferences for Windows

Full Screen preferences affect the default settings for QuickTime Pro's functions when you use View > Full Screen and View > Present Movie. You can also choose when to hide playback controls in Full Screen mode. To open Full Screen preferences, choose Edit > Preferences > Player and click the Full Screen tab.

Choose the default size for movie playback in Full Screen mode. Choices are Half Size, Actual Size, Double Size, Full Screen, and Current Screen. For example, choosing Actual Size will always play the movie at its native resolution, as opposed to scaling it to fit the screen resolution.

Choose the default background color that surrounds movies in full-screen playback.

Select to play in Slideshow mode. A slideshow is controlled using the Left and Right Arrow keys.

Specify whether player controls appear in Full Screen mode.

Choose the amount of time that the player controls are displayed in Full Screen mode before being hidden. The range is from never to 10 seconds.

Recording Preferences for Mac

Recording Preferences for the Mac set options for recording directly into QuickTime Pro using a video camera, iSight, or a microphone. Direct recording is a great option for creating video- or audio-based podcasts and for grabbing video from recorded media for use in other projects.

Choose the video input when recording. Examples are iSight, DV and HDV cameras, and other recognized video cameras attached to the system.

Choose the microphone input device. This could be a built-in microphone, a FireWire input device with a microphone attached, or a USB microphone.

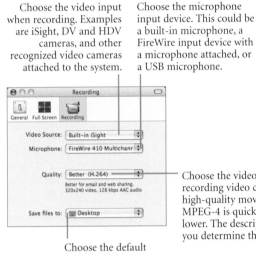

Choose the video compression used when recording video content. H.264 produces very high-quality movies with a small file size. MPEG-4 is quicker, but the quality will be lower. The description below the menu helps you determine the best choice for your needs.

Choose the default location for saving audio and video recordings.

TIP After you've chosen your Video Source and Microphone settings, you need to choose a Quality setting to determine the compression method or codec that will be used when recording QuickTime movies. H.264 provides the best results for podcasts, but you should experiment based on your application and needs. For instance, you might choose Native if you want to capture video at the native resolution of your camera: 720 x 480 for DV cameras and 1080 x 1440 for HDV cameras.

Audio Recording Preferences for Windows

Audio Recording preferences for Windows set options for recording sound directly into QuickTime. Direct recording is a great option for creating audio-based podcasts and for grabbing audio from recorded media for use in other projects. To open Audio Recording preferences, choose Edit > Preferences > Player Preferences and click the Audio Recording tab.

WINDOWS NOTE ▶ Video recording features are not available in Windows.

Click Choose to open Windows Sounds and Audio Devices Properties to enable the microphone input device. Windows lists all available devices in the Sound Recording > Default Device menu.

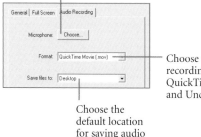

Choose the encoding format used when recording audio content. The formats are QuickTime Movie (.mov), AAC Audio (.m4a), and Uncompressed Audio (.mov).

Choose the default location for saving audio and video recordings.

Using QuickTime Preferences

QuickTime preferences let you set overall playback and recording options. For Mac users, they are actually a part of the Macintosh OS X System Preferences.

Mac users can access QuickTime preferences by choosing QuickTime Player > QuickTime Preferences. QuickTime preferences are organized into five categories: Register, Browser, Update, Streaming, and Advanced.

Windows users open QuickTime preferences by choosing Edit > Preferences > QuickTime Preferences. QuickTime preferences are organized into seven tabs: Register, Audio, Browser, Update, Streaming, File Types, and Advanced.

Register Preferences

Register preferences are used to enter your QuickTime Pro registration key and to verify that you are running QuickTime Pro.

Audio Preferences (Windows only)

The Audio preferences for Windows set options for recording and playback for QuickTime applications.

Click this button to choose the audio devices that Windows will list as available devices in the Sound Recording > Default Device menu.

Select "Safe mode" if you experience audio problems, such as dropout, during playback.

Choose the playback format. Unless you're using a surround-sound setup, the default values are usually acceptable.

Choose the playback device for Musical Instrument Digital Interface (MIDI) files. This setting does not affect playback of standard digital audio files.

Browser Preferences for Mac

Browser preferences are applied to QuickTime movies that are viewed on the Internet using a web browser. They affect QuickTime browser plug-ins when you view content on the web.

Use Brower preferences to set whether movies play automatically and whether they are saved in a cache (temporary memory), so they won't need to be downloaded when replayed on the web.

Determine whether movies begin playing back before they are fully downloaded.

Choose to store movies in a cache (a storage area) so that you don't have to download them every time you want to watch them.

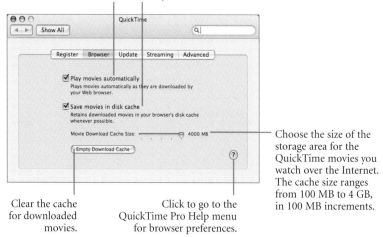

Choose the size of the storage area for the QuickTime movies you watch over the Internet. The cache size ranges from 100 MB to 4 GB, in 100 MB increments.

Clear the cache for downloaded movies.

Click to go to the QuickTime Pro Help menu for browser preferences.

Browser Preferences for Windows

Browser preferences are applied to QuickTime movies that are viewed on the Internet using a web browser. They affect QuickTime browser plug-ins when you view content on the web.

Use Brower preferences to set whether movies play automatically and whether they are saved in a cache (temporary memory), so they won't need to be downloaded when replayed on the web.

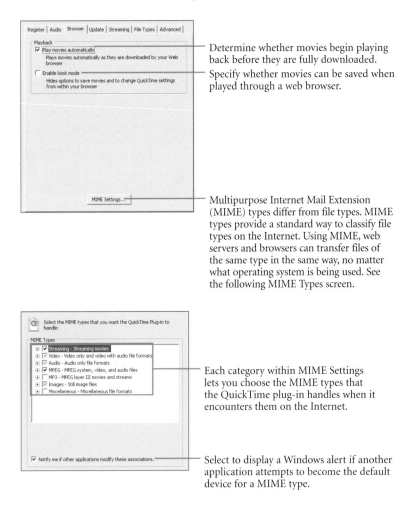

Determine whether movies begin playing back before they are fully downloaded.

Specify whether movies can be saved when played through a web browser.

Multipurpose Internet Mail Extension (MIME) types differ from file types. MIME types provide a standard way to classify file types on the Internet. Using MIME, web servers and browsers can transfer files of the same type in the same way, no matter what operating system is being used. See the following MIME Types screen.

Each category within MIME Settings lets you choose the MIME types that the QuickTime plug-in handles when it encounters them on the Internet.

Select to display a Windows alert if another application attempts to become the default device for a MIME type.

Update Preferences

The Update preferences let you update your QuickTime software and also install additional third-party QuickTime software to extend the functions of QuickTime Pro.

Streaming Preferences for Mac

As with Browser preferences, Streaming preferences affect the way that QuickTime browser plug-ins handle Web content, specifically streaming content. The default streaming speed is Automatic, but you can use the pop-up menu to choose a specific speed based on your connection.

If you know the speed of your connection to the Internet, you can specify it here. You can also set the speed to Automatic, and QuickTime will dynamically determine the speed for the optimal playback of streaming content.

Choose whether streaming content starts playing immediately. Such playback can be problematic when your connection has a lot of congestion; you can turn off this option or tweak it using the Play slider below.

Use this slider to tune Enable Instant-On to include a short delay, which may improve playback during times of Internet congestion.

Click to go to the QuickTime Pro Help menu for Streaming preferences.

Streaming Preferences for Windows

As with Browser preferences, Streaming preferences affect the way that QuickTime browser plug-ins handle Web content, specifically streaming content. The default streaming speed is Automatic, but you can use the pop-up menu to choose a specific speed based on your connection speed.

If you know the speed of your connection to the Internet, you can specify it here. You can also set it to Automatic, and QuickTime will dynamically determine the speed for the optimal playback of streaming content.

Select "Override speed for downloads" and choose from the menu to set a speed specifically for downloading Internet media. This option is available only when Automatic is selected in the Streaming Speed menu. This option is useful for limiting the bandwidth used by content downloads.

Use this option to tune Enable Instant-On to include a short delay, which may improve playeback during times of Internet congestion.

Choose whether streaming content will start playing immediately. Such playback can be problematic when your connection has a lot of congestion; you can turn off this option or tweak it using the Play Streams slider below.

File Types Preferences (Windows only)

File Types preferences are available only in QuickTime Pro for Windows. You can set these preferences to assign QuickTime Pro as the default application for opening and playing a variety of media file types.

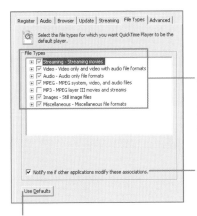

Select the media file types for which QuickTime Pro is the default player application. Click the plus sign (+) to view all available file types. The check is dimmed if file types remain unselected in a category. In general, the default values are acceptable.

Select to display a Windows alert if another application attempts to become the default device for a MIME type.

Click to restore the default file-type assignments.

Advanced Preferences for Mac

Advanced preferences affect the performance and support of the QuickTime browser plug-ins. The main preferences here deal with MIME settings and media keys.

Customize the Internet protocol that QuickTime Pro uses for network connections. You may need to change this setting if you experience problems playing QuickTime content over the Internet.

Choose the MIDI device that will be used to play MIDI data.

Specifiy whether movies can be saved when played through a web browser.

Specify whether QuickTime Pro will play Adobe Flash–based media.

Click to go to the QuickTime Pro Help menu for Advanced preferences.

MIME types differ from file types. MIME types provide a standard way to classify file types on the Internet. Using MIME, web servers and browsers can transfer files of the same type in the same way, no matter what operating system is being used. See the following MIME Types screen.

Media Keys adds keys to QuickTime Pro to access secured media files that have been given to you. Authors provide keys that allow you to unlock and play the file.

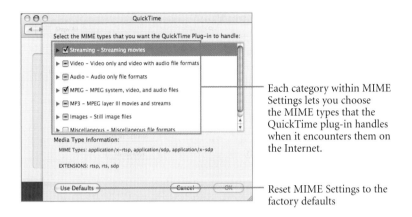

Each category within MIME Settings lets you choose the MIME types that the QuickTime plug-in handles when it encounters them on the Internet.

Reset MIME Settings to the factory defaults

Advanced QuickTime Preferences for Windows

Advanced preferences affect the communication protocols and proxy settings, in addition to cache and video configurations. As with other preferences, the default settings are acceptable in most cases and will not need to be customized.

Customize the Internet protocol that QuickTime Pro uses for network connections. You may need to change this setting if you experience problems playing QuickTime content over the Internet.

Select and enter address and port information to set up the Real Time Streaming Protocol (RTSP) proxy server. Use this option if your firewall is blocking direct Internet access.

Use the slider to set the size of the storage area for the QuickTime movies you download over the Internet. The cache size ranges from 0 to 10 GB. Click Empty Cache to clear the cache contents.

Select "Safe mode" only if you experience problems displaying images or video in QuickTime Pro. Before selecting Safe mode, be sure you have installed the latest Windows videos drivers for your system. In most cases, the default DirectX options are the best choices.

Select to enable DirectDraw and video acceleration under DirectX on the primary and the secondary monitor (when present). By default, all options are selected (recommended).

Media Keys adds keys to QuickTime Pro to access secured media files that have been given to you. Authors provide keys that allow you to unlock and play the file.

Select to display the QuickTime application icon in the system tray. When this option is selected, you can double-click the tray icon to launch QuickTime Pro, and you can right-click it to view a menu of QuickTime functions.

Glossary

2:35:1 aspect ratio   A common widescreen aspect ratio used in theatrical-release motion pictures.

3:2 aspect ratio   The common aspect ratio of digital video (DV) and DVD.

3:2 pulldown   A technique to convert between film footage frame rates and video footage frame rates.

4:3 aspect ratio   The common aspect ratio of an NTSC standard-definition television set.

16:9 aspect ratio   The common aspect ratio of a high-definition television set and HD video formats.

16 bit   A standard bit depth for digital audio recording and playback.

animation codec   Lossless codec used for real-time play-back of uncompressed RGB video.

AppleScript   Scripting language developed by Apple Computer that can send commands to scriptable applications and create simple instruction sets that can be packaged into executable files.

Apple Intermediate Codec   A high-quality video codec developed by Apple for use as an alternative to native MPEG-2 HDV editing in an HDV workflow. Instead of editing the MPEG-2 HDV data directly, this codec captures video from a tape source and then transcodes it to optimize the video data for playback performance and quality.

A

aspect ratio The ratio between the width and height of an image. For example, standard-definition TV has an aspect ratio of 4:3; high-definition TV has a 16:9 aspect ratio.

B

bandwidth A measurement of the amount of information delivered from a source to a destination within a period of time. Bandwidth is generally stated in kilobits per second (kbps) or megabits per second (mbps).

bit budgeting The process of calculating the required data rates of media to determine whether it will fit within a specific bandwidth or within the limitations of a distribution format.

bit rate A measure of the quantity of data transmitted over time. *See also* bandwidth.

broadband A relative term used to identify the faster data delivery options provided by Internet service providers.

C

codec Abbreviation for *compression/decompression*. A program used to compress and decompress data such as audio and video files.

compression The process by which data files (often video, graphics, and audio data) are reduced in size. The size reduction of an audio or video file implemented by removing perceptually redundant image data is referred to as a *lossy* compression scheme. A *lossless* compression scheme uses a mathematical process to reduce file size by consolidating redundant information without discarding it.

data rate   The speed at which data is transferred, often described in megabytes per second (Mbps). Higher video data rates usually exhibit increased visual quality, but higher data rates also require more system resources (processor speed, hard disk space, and performance) to process. Some codecs allow you to specify a maximum data rate for a media capture. *See also* bandwidth; bit rate.

D

deinterlace   The process of combining video frames composed of two interlaced fields into a single unified frame.

digital video   Video that has been captured, manipulated, and stored in a digital format, and that can be easily imported into a computer. Digital video formats include Digital-8, DVC Pro, DVCAM, and DV.

DV   A standardized digital video format created by a consortium of camcorder vendors that uses Motion JPEG compression in a 720 x 480 resolution running at 29.97 frames per second (NTSC), or a 720 x 546 resolution running at 25 frames per second (PAL). DV content is stored at a bit rate of 25 MB per second with a compression of 4:1:1.

field dominance   The choice of whether field 1 or field 2 will first be displayed on a monitor. The default value should be Lower (even) for DV and Targa captures.

F

floating point   A system of calculation that allows otherwise fixed incremental measurements within a bit depth to change in relative fashion so that a higher degree of accuracy can be achieved at the widest dynamic ranges.

frame rate The playback speed of the individual images in a moving sequence, either film or video, and measured in frames per second (fps). Film in 16mm or 35mm is usually shot at 24 fps, NTSC video at 29.97 fps, and PAL video at 25 fps. HD can employ a variety of frame rates depending on the format.

H

HD (high definition) High-definition formats were created to increase the number of pixels (resolution) of video images, as well as to solve many of the frame rate and cadence problems between film and video. The two most common resolutions for HD footage are 1080, with a native resolution of 1920 x 1080, and 720, with a native resolution of 1280 x 720. Both formats can have various frame rates and be interlaced or progressive.

I

I frame *See* keyframe.

interlaced video A video scanning method that first scans the odd-numbered picture lines (field 1) and then scans the even-numbered picture lines (field 2). The two fields are sequenced together to constitute a single frame of video.

K

keyframe A point at which a filter, motion effect, or audio level changes value. There must be at least two keyframes representing two different values to constitute a change.

L

lossless compression *See* compression.

lossy compression *See* compression.

M

metadata Information contained within a digital file that further explains the content or context of the media.

MPEG Acronym for *Moving Pictures Experts Group*. Also, a group of compression standards for video and audio developed by that group, which includes MPEG-1, MPEG-2, MPEG-1 Layer 3 (MP3), and MPEG-4.

multiplexed   Also called *muxing*. The interleaving of audio and video into one stream.

muxing   *See* multiplexed.

NTSC   Acronym for *National Television Systems Committee*. Also, a standard format for color TV broadcasting developed by the committee and used mainly in North America, Mexico, and Japan. The NTSC format consists of 525 scan lines per frame, at a resolution of 720 x 486 pixels (720 x 480 for DV), running at a 29.97 fps.

N

PAL   Acronym for *phase alternating line*. A European color TV broadcasting standard consisting of 625 lines per frame, 720 x 546 pixels per frame, running at 25 fps.

P

pixel   Abbreviation for *picture element*. One dot in a video or still image.

pixel aspect ratio   The width-to-height ratio for the pixels that comprise an image. Pixels on computer screens and in high-definition video signals are square (1:1 ratio). Pixels in standard-definition video signals are not square (0.9:1 ratio).

progressive frame video   Also called *progressive scan*. A format for delivering video in which all lines are drawn in sequence. It is commonly denoted with the letter *p*: for instance, 720p.

progressive scan   *See* progressive frame video.

RAID   Acronym for *redundant array of independent discs*. A high-performance, high-capacity data storage technology often used with nonlinear editing systems that configures a group of hard disks to act as one large drive volume.

R

RGB   Acronym for *red-green-blue*, the three primary colors that make up a color image.

S

sample rate The frequency at which analog audio is monitored and converted into digital information. The sampling rate of an audio stream specifies how often digital samples are captured. Higher sample rates yield higher-quality audio. Standard audio sampling rates are usually measured in kilohertz (kHz). The standard CD sampling rate is 44.1 kHz. A rate of 48 kHz is also common in professional audio production.

SD (standard definition) The term used to differentiate traditional television broadcast resolutions from those of the high-definition formats. Standard-definition broadcast resolutions are 720 x 486 (NTSC) and 720 x 576 (for PAL). *See also HD.*

T

TIFF Acronym for *tagged image file format.* A bitmapped graphics file format for monochrome, grayscale, and 8- and 24-bit color images. There are two types of TIFF images: with an alpha channel and without an alpha channel.

timecode A numbering system of electronic signals that is placed on video content and used to identify individual video frames. Each video frame is labeled with hours, minutes, seconds, and frames, expressed in the format 01:00:00:00. Timecode can be drop-frame, non-drop-frame, or time-of-day (TOD) timecode, or European Broadcast Union (EBU) for PAL projects.

X

XSAN Apple Computer's branded, cross-platform storage area network (SAN) solution that offers both high speed and large storage capacity.

Y

YUV The three-channel PAL video signal with one luminance (Y) and two chrominance color difference signals (UV).

Index

Numbers

2:35:1 aspect ratio, 127
3:2 aspect ratio, 127
3:2 pulldown, 127
4:3 aspect ratio, 127
16-bit, 32, 127
16:9 aspect ratio, 127
48 kHz source rate, 25, 32, 132

A

A/V controls, 107–108
AAC (Advanced Audio Coding) codec, 33–34, 99
.aif files, 34
alpha channels, 23, 70
Animation codec, 22–25, 99, 127
Apple Intermediate codec, 127
Apple Internet resources, 103
Apple Pixlet Video codec, 99
Apple TV, 21–22
AppleScript, 127
architecture of QuickTime, 1
aspect ratios, 127, 128, 131
audio
 AAC codec, 33–34
 Audio Meter, 13
 capturing with Mac, 9–11, 12
 capturing with Windows, 13
 CD sampling rates, 32
 exporting to 48kHz AIFF, 32
 meter settings for, 10
 Player recording preferences (Windows), 117
 QuickTime preferences (Windows), 118
 sampling rate of audio streams, 32
 3G settings and movie delivery, 93
Audio Meter, 13
autoloading web pages, 60–63
Automator, 84–85
AVC (Advanced Video Codec). *See* H.264 codec

B

bandwidth, 128
bit budgeting, 128
bit rate, 128
broadband, 128
bugs, graphic, 47–50

C

cache, 119, 120, 125
cameras, 11, 12
CDs, audio sampling rates, 32
cellular phones and movie delivery, 88–95
 3G audio settings, 93
 3G formats and platforms, 89
 3G settings, advanced, 95
 3G streaming settings, 94
 3G text settings, 94
 3G video settings, 90–92
 3GPP protocols, 88
CGI environments, 22–23, 31
chapter tracks and interactivity, 68–69
Cinepak, 100
clickable web links and interactivity, 64–67

codecs, 20, 128
  AAC, 33–34, 99
  Animation, 22–25, 99, 127
  Apple Pixlet Video, 99
  Cinepak, 100
  DV/DVCPRO-NTSC, 100
  DVCPRO 50, 100
  DVCPRO HD, 100
  exporting movies with, 22–29
  H.264, 11, 16, 21, 26–29, 92, 100, 116
  importance of, 42
  Internet resources, 103
  Linear PCM, 25, 32, 101
  Motion JPEG, 101
  MPEG-4, 3, 11, 81, 84, 92, 101
  PAL, 100
  Photo-JPEG, 101
  Planar RGB, 101
  Q-Design Music 2, 101
  Qualcomm Pure Voice, 101
  Sorenson 3, 102
  third-party, 3, 19, 34–35
  TIFF, 47, 102, 132
  Uncompressed 8/10 bit, 102
combining movies, 54–55
compatibility and plug-ins, 34–35
compression, 11, 128. *See also* codecs;
    exporting movies
Compression Type function, 24, 27, 30
container files, 19, 42, 59
copyright notices, 41–42
cross-platform workflow, 19–21
custom skins and interactivity, 70–76

D

data rates, 128, 129
  Animation codec, 99
  hint tracks, 83
  MPEG-4, 101
  in podcasting, 34
  size *vs.* quality, 28
  Uncompressed 8/10 bit, 102
deinterlace, 25, 129
deleting parts of a movie, 53–54

delivering movies, 79–98
  to cellular phones, 88–95
  hint tracks, 81–87
  progressive download, 80
  QuickTime Broadcaster (Mac),
    95–98
  real-time streaming, 81–84
Device Native, 11, 12
digital video, 129
.Mac email accounts, 15, 17–18
downloading movies from Internet, 15
drag-and-drop editing, 56–57
DV, 129
DV NTSC video, 19, 20
DV/DVCPRO-NTSC, 100
DVCPRO 50, 100
DVCPRO HD, 100

E

editing movies, 37–58
  basic editing, 50–57
  changing names, 40
  combining, 54–55
  copyright notices, 41–42
  deleting parts of, 53–54
  displaying information, 38
  drag-and-drop, 56–57
  graphic bugs, 47–50
  properties, 38–42
  removing frames, 54
  Selection & Scale, 45–46
  selections, 51–53
  tracks, 42–50
Email function
  .Mac email accounts, 15, 17–18
  compressed formats and delivery, 11
  H.264 codec, 16–17
  sharing movies, 16–17
exporting audio to 48 kHz AIFF, 32
exporting movies, 19–36
  AAC codec, 33–34
  Animation codec, 22–25
  for Apple TV, 21–22
  48 kHz AIFF audio, 32

image sequences, 31
for iPod with video, 20–21
podcasting with AAC, 34
still images, 30–31
third-party codecs, 34–35
using H.264, 21, 26–29

F

field dominance, 129
film production, 22–23
Final Cut Studio, 1, 2, 14, 32, 42, 100, 109
Flash Video, 34
Flip4Mac plug-in, 35
floating point, 129
.flv files, 34
Frame Rate function, 130
  in animated slideshows, 77
  exporting movies and, 24, 27
frames, removing, 54
Full Screen mode, 5–7

G

GarageBand, 69
graphic bugs, 47–50

H

H.264 codec, 100
  Email function, 16–17
  exporting movies with, 21, 26–29
  podcasting, 116
  recording movies, 11
  video encoding, 89, 92
HD (high definition), 20, 130
Hint Exporter Settings, 82
hint tracks, 81–87
HomePage feature, sharing movies,
  17–18

I

I frames. *See* keyframes
image sequences
  in animated slideshows, 76–78
  exporting, 31

interactive movies, 59–78
  autoloading web pages, 60–63
  chapter tracks, 68–69
  clickable web links, 64–67
  custom skins, 70–76
  slideshows from image sequences,
    76–78
interlaced video, 130
Internet resources, 103–104
Internet, downloading movies from, 15
iPod, exporting movies to, 20–21
iTunes, 33

K

Key Frames function, 24, 27, 28
keyboard shortcuts, QuickTime
  Player, 110
keyframes, 24, 27, 28, 130

L

layering effects, 42–44
Linear PCM, 25, 32, 101
logos, 47–50
lossless compression, 11, 128
lossless production, 22–23
lossy compression, 11, 128

M

.m4v file extension, 21
.Mac email accounts, 15, 17–18
markers, chapter, 68–69
metadata, 14, 130
microphone settings, 9–13, 116–117
MIME (Multipurpose Internet Mail
  Extension), 120, 125
Motion JPEG, 101, 129
Movie Info function, 38
Movie Properties
  chapter tracks, 69
  clickable web links, 67
  copyright notices, 41–42
  custom skins, 74–75
  display names, 40

Movie Properties *(continued)*
  during editing, 40–42
  logos, 49
  tracks, 38–39
  web page autoloading, 63
movie tracks, 42–50, 59
  add to Selection & Scale, 45–46
  adding tracks from another movie,
    42–44
  chapter tracks, 68–69
  graphic bugs, 47–50
  hint tracks, 81–87
  movie properties, 38–39
  movie tracks, 59
movies
  combining, 54–55
  deleting parts of, 53–54
  delivering. *See* delivering movies
  editing. *See* editing movies
  exporting. *See* exporting movies
  interactive. *See* interactive movies
  recording, 9–13
  saving, 14–15
  sharing, 15–18
MP3 files, 32
MPEG, 130
MPEG-4, 3, 11, 81, 84, 92, 101, 130.
  See also H.264 codec
multi-movie playback, 7–8
multiplexed, 131
muxing, 131

N
New Movie Recording command, 12
NTSC (National Television Systems
  Committee), 131

P
PAL (phase alternating line), 100, 131
phones. *See* cellular phones and movie
  delivery
Photo-JPEG, 101
PICT format, 47

pixel aspect ratio, 131
pixels, 131
Planar RGB, 101
playback options, 4, 7–8, 25, 52, 118
playing movies, 3–8
plug-ins and compatibility, 34–35
podcasting, 20–21, 34, 116
preferences. *See* QuickTime Player;
  QuickTime preferences
Present Movie function, 106
progressive download and movie
  delivery, 80
progressive frame video, 131
progressive scan, 131
properties. *See* Movie Properties
PSD format, 47

Q
Q-Design Music 2, 101
Qualcomm Pure Voice, 101
QuickTime Broadcaster (Mac), 95–98
QuickTime Player
  A/V controls, 107–108
  Audio Recording preferences
    (Windows), 117
  editing features, 37
  Full Screen preferences (Mac),
    113–114
  Full Screen preferences (Windows),
    115
  General preferences, 112–113
  H.264 codec and exporting, 17, 26
  keyboard shortcuts, 110
  overview, 105–106
  Present Movie function, 106
  Recording preferences (Mac), 116
  software upgrades, 108–109
QuickTime preferences, 111–126
  Advanced (Mac), 124–125
  Advanced (Windows), 125–126
  Audio (Windows), 118
  Browser (Mac), 119
  Browser (Windows), 119–120
  File Types (Windows), 123

Player, 112–117
Register, 118
Streaming (Mac), 121
Streaming (Windows), 122
Update, 121
QuickTime Pro overview, 1–18
architecture of, 1
capturing audio only (Mac), 9–11
capturing audio only (Windows), 13
capturing video and audio (Mac), 11–12
Full Screen mode, 5–7
Full Screen preferences (Windows), 7
movie playback options, 4
multi-movie playback, 7–8
playing movies, 3–8
recording movies, 9–13
saving movies, 14–15
sharing movies, 15–18
sharing movies and email, 16–17
sharing movies to HomePage, 17–18
standard player controls, 5
QVGA frame size, 29

R

RAID (redundant array of independent discs), 131
Real Time Streaming Protocol (RTSP), 81, 125
RealPlayer, 3, 34
real-time streaming, 81–84
recording movies, 9–13
reference files, 14
removing a frame, 54
RGB (red-green-blue), 132
.rm files, 3, 34

S

sample rate, 132
samples, 59
saving movies, 14–15
scripting process, 60
scripting software, third-party, 104
SD (standard definition), 132

SDP (Session Description Protocol), 97–98
Selection & Scale function
clickable web links, 66
custom skins, 73
movie tracks, 45–46
web page autoloading, 62
self-contained files, 14, 50, 80
Share feature, 15–18
sharing movies, 15–18
skins, custom, 70–76
slideshows, 76–78
software upgrades, 2, 108–109
Sorenson 3, 102
SoundTrack Pro, 9
standard player controls, 5
still images, 30–31
streaming content, 15, 32, 81–84, 94, 121, 122, 125. *See also* QuickTime Broadcaster (Mac)
syntax, 61

T

tags, adding, 56–57
Third Generation Partnership Project (3GPP) protocol, 88. *See also* 3G protocol and movie delivery
third-party codecs, 3, 19, 34–35. *See also* codecs
third-party scripting software, 104
third-party video cameras, 12
3G protocol and movie delivery
advanced settings, 95
audio settings, 93
formats and platforms, 89, 95
streaming settings, 94
text settings, 94
video settings, 90–92
TIFF (tagged image file format), 47, 102, 132
Tiger. *See* Automator
timecode, 132
tracks. *See* movie tracks
transcoding. *See* exporting movies

U

Uncompressed 8/10 bit, 102

V

video
  Apple Pixlet Video codec, 99
  cameras, 11, 12
  capturing with Mac, 11–12
  cellular phones, 3G settings for,
      90–92
  digital, 129
  DV NTSC, 19, 20
  encoding, 89, 92
  exporting movies to iPods, 20–21
  Flash Video, 34
  interlaced, 130
  progressive frame video, 131
  video formats, 92
  Windows, lack of recording
      features, 13

W

.wav files, 34
web links, clickable, 64–67
web pages
  autoloading, 60–63
  clickable web links and interactivity,
      64–67
  frame sizes, 29
Windows
  capturing audio only, 13
  Full Screen mode, 7
  Full Screen Player preferences, 115
  lack of video recording features, 13
  Player recording preferences, 117
  QuickTime preferences, 118–120,
      122, 123, 125–126
  Windows Media, 3, 34, 35
wiring, 60
.wmv files, 34

X

XSAN, 132

Y

YUV, 132